Immorality in the Church

Can We Sweep It under the Rug?

Immorality in the Church
Can We Sweep It under the Rug?

An Exegetical Commentary on
First Corinthians Five

By
Spiros Zodhiates, Th.D.

AMG
PUBLISHERS
Chattanooga, TN 37422

Immorality in the Church

Can We Sweep It under the Rug?

An Exegetical Commentary on First Corinthians Five

ISBN 0-89957-471-8

Printed in the United States of America
03 02 01 00 99 98 –A– 7 6 5 4 3 2

To Dr. Wayne A. Barber, my beloved pastor and a brilliant student of the Greek New Testament.

Contents

Preface

Immorality in the church is not a modern phenomenon. It is as ancient as the church established by the apostle Paul at Corinth.

Human nature has not changed. No individual who believes in Jesus Christ becomes sinless (Rom. 7:20; 1 John 1:9, 10). He continues to live under the influences of a world that is full of sin (1 John 5:19).

In His high-priestly prayer, our Lord prayed for His own redeemed people, "I pray not that thou should take them out of the world, but that thou should keep them from the evil" (John 17:15). Jesus recognized and showed concern that we as believers are under the attack of the evil one. We need to be always on our guard and given to God's Word for the victory needed (John 17:17).

The greatest of the apostles, Paul, recognized not only the evil around him, but also the presence of sin within his flesh. He stated, "Now if I do that I would not, it is no more I that do it, but sin that dwelleth in me" (Rom. 7:20). He was honest enough to confess that sin dwelt within him and that all of us are faced with a tremendous struggle.

But on the other hand, victory is promised! The same apostle who acknowledged the presence of sin also triumphantly said, "We are more than conquerors through Him that loved us" (Rom. 8:37). He included us as victors with Him.

In the fifth chapter of 1 Corinthians we are shown how Paul handled a case of incest in the Corinthian church, a church that he had established (Acts 18:1–17; 1 Cor. 4:14–16). To our knowledge, there has never been a thorough exegetical study which English readers could easily understand of this difficult chapter from the Greek text.

It is this lack which, by God's enablement, we have tried to fill, as for other portions of First Corinthians:

A Richer Life for You in Christ (1 Cor. 1)

A Revolutionary Mystery (1 Cor. 2)

Getting the Most Out of Life (1 Cor. 3)

You and Public Opinion (1 Cor. 4:1–5)

Formula for Happiness (1 Cor. 4:6–21)

May I Divorce and Remarry? (1 Cor. 7)

The Gifts of The Holy Spirit and the Holy Spirit's Baptism and Infilling (1 Cor. 12:1–13)

Variety in Christ's Body and the Better Gifts of the Holy Spirit (1 Cor. 12:14–31)

To Love Is to Live (1 Cor. 13)

Tongues !? (1 Cor. 14:1–33)

Conquering the Fear of Death (1 Cor. 15).

To these eleven volumes we now add volume twelve dealing with First Corinthians chapter five entitled *Immorality in the Church: Can We Sweep it Under the Rug?*

May we ask you to pray for us as we continue to study First Corinthians, realizing that what Paul wrote to the church in Corinth addresses almost exactly the same problems and concerns of the church of the twentieth century. The temptations of the first century are present today, and we believe even much more prevalent, but the cure remains the same. Let us study Paul's diagnostic and therapeutic principles. My prayer is that we may experience the same power that is in the blood of Jesus Christ to cleanse us from all unrighteousness (1 John 1:9). He will exercise His cleansing power if we sincerely confess our sins and by His grace obey Him.

SPIROS ZODHIATES

An Overview of First Corinthians

Author:	Paul the apostle, author of thirteen other epistles to various individuals and congregations.
Date:	About A.D. 55.
Recipients:	The congregation Paul had established in Corinth.
Place:	From Ephesus
Theme:	Paul had received news about the Corinthian brethren from several sources (1 Cor. 1:11; 7:1; 16:17). The church was afflicted with many of the problems that face young churches and new converts. The apostle, under the inspiration of the Holy Spirit, decided to write this urgent letter to admonish and instruct the church. Among other topics he discussed: the necessity of church discipline (5:1–13); divisions and disputes among Christians (1:10–16; 6:1–11); matters of conscience (8:1–13; 10:19–33); the support of preachers (9:1–27); abuses of the Lord's Supper (10:16–17, 21; 11:17–34); the misuse of spiritual gifts (12:1—14:40); and the importance of the resurrection of Jesus Christ (15:1–58).

An Outline of First Corinthians

In the days of the apostle Paul, Corinth was the capital city of the Roman province of Achaia and the glory of Greece. Though its great ancient splendor had been destroyed by the Romans in 120 B.C., the city was rebuilt under Julius Caesar and restored to wealth and luxury under Augustus. Among all the cities of the world, however, it was most well known for its lewdness. The apostle Paul lived in Corinth for eighteen months (Acts 18:11). After his departure, Paul went to Ephesus. During his three-year stay there, he heard reports of wickedness and division within the Corinthian church. In an effort to correct these evils, Paul wrote several letters to them, including the epistle of First Corinthians.

1:1–9	The introductory remarks of Paul.
1:10–16	Paul condemns the divisions in the church and exhorts its members to unity.
1:17—2:16	Paul defends his ministry. He has preached the wisdom of Christ crucified. This wisdom is foolishness to the world, but is the glory of all those to whom the Spirit of God has revealed the truthfulness of it.
3:1–5	Paul declares that the simplicity of his teaching was due to the carnal state of the Corinthians, which state is clearly evidenced by their divisions.
3:6–23	Jesus Christ is the only foundation. Ministers are mere servants; the work is God's.
4:1–6	The duty of ministers is faithfulness.
4:6–21	Paul contrasts the arrogance and conceit of the false teachers to the humility and sacrifice of the apostles. Using his unique position as their spiritual father, Paul calls on the Corinthian believers to be discerning.
5:1–13	Flagrant, sexual immorality was being practiced by one of the members of the congregation. Paul reproves

	their lack of discipline and calls for expulsion of the guilty party.
6:1–11	Christians should not bring their legal disputes before heathen judges.
6:12–20	Paul reprimands the perversion of the principle of Christian liberty to excuse fornication. Our bodies belong to the Lord and should be devoted to His glory.
7:1–17	Paul answers questions about marriage.
7:18–24	Paul advises that, provided they are not immoral or unlawful, our social positions should remain intact after coming to Christ.
7:25–40	Paul answers questions about virgins and widows.
8:1–13	Christian liberty and conscience: was it lawful to eat meat that had been sacrificed to false gods?
9:1–23	Paul declares the right of ministers to be faithfully supported by their congregation.
9:24—10:13	Exhortations to self-denial.
10:14—11:1	While the purchase of meat offered to idols is a matter of conscience, attendance at the heathen feasts of sacrifice is idolatry, even if such was not their intention.
11:2–16	Men and women should take care to conform to the customs of dress in their community that assure modesty and properly reflect the man to be "the glory of God" and the woman to be "the glory of the man."
11:17–34	Paul exhorts the Corinthians to properly partake of the Lord's Supper.
12:1–31	Paul answers their questions about spiritual gifts. He reminds them that they are all members of one body. God has distributed these gifts so that each member may perform the function it is designed for.

13:1–13	Love [*agápe* {26}] is superior to all other gifts.
14:1–25	The gift of prophecy is more valuable than the gift of tongues.
14:26–40	Principles for orderly public worship.
15:1–34	Paul proves the resurrection of Christ is fact. It is the foundation of our faith and the surety of our resurrection.
15:35–58	Paul explains the nature of our resurrection.
16:1–9	Paul's specific instructions for the collection of monies from several Greek congregations for the poverty-stricken saints in Palestine.
16:10–12	Recommendations for Timothy and Apollos to be accepted by the Corinthians.
16:13–24	Paul's final admonition to them to stand firm in the faith. Salutation.

1 Cor. 5:1 | *Sin in the Local Church*

It is reported commonly that there is fornication among you, and such fornication as is not so much as named among the Gentiles, that one should have his father's wife.

The Corinthian church was by no means a pure church, but it had among its members some who were exceptionally gifted. The sins of the flesh had overcome a few individuals in the church, but such sinners did not leave the church; they continued to attend and be counted as Christians. The Corinthian church was a compromising church. Not only did it exist in a sinful environment, but it allowed the sinful world to freely penetrate it. Sin in the Corinthian church was an open and accepted way of life.

Secret and Public Sin

Sin among the Christian community may be secret or out in the open. If the pastor of a local church learns about a secret sin in his congregation, he should not imprudently publicize it. The publicizing of sin within the church or beyond its borders is not the duty of any Christian, and especially not of a church leader. One should carefully examine his or her motive for wanting to expose a fellow believer's sin. If it becomes necessary to expose an offense, the chief purpose should be to reclaim the offender.

Soul-Searching Questions

There are two considerations which should guide every action of the believer: the way it will affect someone else, and the way it will affect the cause of Christ. Before exposing another's sin, there are certain questions one must consider.

First, is the desire to reveal another's sin redemptive in purpose, or is it merely to expose his or her weakness in comparison to one's own spirituality? Telling the truth is the Christian's duty, but it becomes a sin when the motive is wrong. If it is not spoken in love, truth is not an implement for corrective surgery, but a weapon for killing the patient. Therefore, whenever we are tempted to speak about the unknown or little-known sin of another, we should ask ourselves what good, if any, will be accomplished by revealing that sin. Finding fault is easy; correcting it is difficult. Criticism for its own sake is wrong, but loving and gentle criticism in an effort to correct the behavior of others is a Christian virtue. The motive makes all the difference.

A bright lad had his dog hitched to a lawn mower to pull it while he guided it. As someone passed by, the dog stopped to bark. The boy assured the pedestrian, "Don't mind the dog, he is just looking for an excuse to rest. It is easier to bark than to pull the mower." How true the boy's remark was. We must be careful about barking at those who cross our path. It is easier to be publicly critical than privately corrective. And it is invariably more difficult, if not impossible, to correct someone after we have taken the liberty to publicize his or her sin. Faultfinding is as dangerous as it is easy. It is much less difficult to destroy a reputation than to reconstruct a character torn down by thoughtless gossip.

The second question we should ask ourselves when we become aware of the secret sin of another is whether it will help or harm the cause of Christ if it is publicized. Neither personal vindication nor redressing our grievances is sufficient reason to expose another's sin. Personal injury should not be used as an excuse for an impulsive act of revenge.

When Ole Bull, the great Norwegian violinist, was in the United States, he was assailed by much hostile criticism. James Gordon Bennett offered him space in the *New York Herald* to reply to his critics. In broken English he declined the editor's offer, saying, "I tink, Mr. Bennett, it is best tey writes against me and I play against tem."

What was the Lord Jesus' most eloquent defense against the Pharisees? It was His deeds. When fellow Christians err, we must not hasten to publicize it, but rather seek, prayerfully and gently, to redeem them.

In First Corinthians 6 Paul deals with the solution of disputes among Christians within the context of the local Christian community. In trying to redress the wrong, Paul points out that our own interests should not be the major consideration. He asks, "Why do you not rather take wrong? Why do you not rather suffer yourselves to be defrauded?" (v. 7). The Greek word is *adikeísthe*, meaning "to suffer injustice" or "to be treated unjustly." Paul says that we must allow ourselves to suffer an injustice rather than cause someone else to become irreconcilable to virtue or to bring reproach upon the name of Jesus Christ. Our first concern in dealing with another's wrongdoing should be the advancement of God's kingdom and not our own personal interests.

Paul does not at any cost cover up sin where it is found. He exposes it when such exposure is necessary to bring correction. The fifth chapter of First Corinthians contains his exposure of the sin of fornication as it manifested itself in an individual family. He begins his discourse by saying, "It is reported commonly that there is fornication among you, and such fornication as is not so much as named among the Gentiles, that one should have his father's wife." In Greek the verse begins with the adverb *hólōs*. The same adverb is used in Matthew 5:34: "But I say unto you, swear not at all." That expression "at all" is *hólōs*. The word is also used in 1 Corinthians 6:7: "Now therefore there is utterly [*hólōs*] a fault among you." This means there is a fault among you about the sinfulness of which there is no doubt. It is an undisputed fault. This adverb *hólōs* is also used in 1 Corinthians 15:29: "Else what shall they do which are baptized for the dead, if the dead rise not at all [*hólōs*]?" Here the adverb means "under any circumstances." Thus we conclude that the adverb in 1 Corinthians 5:1 makes it clear that what was going on in the Corinthian church had ceased to be a private matter. It became commonly known. That seems to be Paul's concern. It did not become known to every single person because this would have been expressed with the dative plural of the adjective *hólois*, meaning to all people. It rather means that this sin of fornication became the common gossip of the town. Anything evil becomes news. It was so in Corinth; it is so today.

Were there good things that were taking place in Corinth? Of course there were. But the evil that was perpetrated among the members of just one family took wings as it was announced from the housetops. We Christians should be extremely careful of our conduct, because our sin is not a purely private affair. It becomes public before we know it, and affects the whole church. One little mosquito bite or bee sting or sliver in the flesh brings the complete attention of the whole body. Our good is only slightly recognized, but our evil is readily and commonly spoken about. It can never be kept a secret.

Incest, the Talk of the Town

The Greek text of this verse begins with the adverb *hólōs*, the translation of which is somewhat controversial. Some translate it "actually" (NASB, NIV, NKJV). The King James Version, however, has it more correctly rendered "commonly." This adverb is derived from *hólos*, an adjective meaning whole, all, including every part.

As an adverb, *hólōs* is more commonly used in compounds in a negative sense meaning "not at all" as in Matthew 5:34, "Swear not at all"; 1 Corinthians 6:7, "there is utterly [totally] a fault among you"; and in 1 Corinthians 15:29, "if the dead rise not at all."

The News of Sin Spreads Fast and Affects Many

In our study, we find that 1 Corinthians 5:1 is the only instance in the New Testament in which the adverb is used in a positive sense. If Paul wanted to stress the reality of the report versus its being only a rumor, he would have used a far more common Greek word, *óntōs*, which means "indeed, in actuality." (The word *óntōs* is used in Mark 11:32; Luke 23:47; 24:34; John 8:36; 1 Cor. 14:25; Gal. 3:21; 2 Pet. 2:18, etc.). Since he mentions a specific case of incest, there is no reason for him to say "actually" or "in reality." That a certain man was having sexual relations with his father's wife was a fact widely known and commonly talked about, to the shame of the church in Corinth. As lexicographer Edward Robinson says, "The word *hólōs* means everywhere, generally." The fact that this sinful state was widely known in Corinth, and very possibly elsewhere, only served to compound the evil, for it brought shame on the cause of Christ.

Publicity of Sin in the Church Spells Urgency

"Generally [or widely] it is heard that there is fornication among you." What a terrible indictment by Paul who was the first to proclaim the gospel to the Corinthians (Acts 18:1–17)! He felt a sense of shame that his own children in the faith had fallen to such immorality. Sin can seldom be kept within closed boundaries. Its notoriety and harm spread like wildfire. It is typically the bad news that gets publicity, not the good news. Paul wished that this bad news had not been so widely published, and the urgency of dealing with the matter was due to the general knowledge of it. He does not ask them to wait until he has had the opportunity to come among them; he tells them that they must join with his spirit although he is absent (v. 4) in order to correct the disorder immediately.

Paul's directive, however, does not give us the dubious privilege of hanging out our dirty clothes on a public line. Our sinning brother is part of our own body since we are all one in Christ. In exposing our brother, therefore, we are harming the whole body of Christ. It is so much better to deal with such evil in circumspect privacy. Let us remember that when an individual in a Christian community does something wrong and that wrong is publicized, even if the individual is restored, the stain on the Christian community remains.

In Matthew 18:15–17, the Lord taught that first a personal encounter with the offender must be made, and if that is unsuccessful, a second encounter in the presence of two witnesses. If this did not lead to repentance, then the matter was to be brought to the whole church. However, in Matthew, it is a matter of one brother wronging another, while in 1 Corinthians 5 we have a sin perpetrated by an individual which tarnishes the witness of the whole church. The harm was done not to a particular person, but to the whole congregation and, by extension, to the cause of Christ in general.

In 1 Corinthians 6:9, 10, Paul delineates some who are not going to inherit the kingdom of God. He lists categories such as fornicators, idolaters, adulterers, effeminate, abusers of themselves with mankind (that is homosexuals), thieves, covetous, drunkards, revilers, and extortioners. What does he do then? Name such sinners? Did he know who belonged to these categories of sinful practices? Most likely he did. However, instead of naming the sinners, he simply says in verse eleven ". . . and such were some of you." He gives no names.

However, in writing to Timothy, Paul did not hesitate to mention names when it came to those who were proponents of erroneous doctrine. In 2 Timothy 2:16–18 he writes, "But shun profane and vain babblings: for they will increase unto more ungodliness and their word will eat as does a canker: of whom is Hymenaeus and Philetus; who concerning the truth have erred, saying that the resurrection is past already; and overthrow the faith of some." Here he names two who taught that the resurrection was already past. Hymenaeus was a harmful teacher associated with Alexander whom both, insofar as faith is concerned, suffered shipwreck and whom Paul delivered to Satan (1 Tim. 1:19, 20). Such delivery to Satan may take the form of bodily punishment (cf. 1 Cor. 5:5; Job 2:6).

The instances of church or apostolic discipline in which individuals are named are related to an infringement on the truth, the faith, or the Christian doctrine, rather than a moral aberration as such. The error of Hymenaeus and Philetus was the spiritualization of the resurrection.

In Acts 5:3–11 we have punishment imposed upon Ananias and Sapphira. Their sin was that of lying in order to appear more generous than they actually were. That sin did not concern their bodies but their disposition toward the Holy Spirit.

In Acts 8:18–24 we find a sorcerer, Simon the magician, trying to buy the gift of the Holy Spirit with money. One of the basic doctrines of the New Testament is that the mystical and miraculous relationship of man with God cannot be acquired by any physical act of man or any material thing he can offer

(Luke 11:37–42). Peter, in unequivocal condemnation, said to him, "Your heart is not right in the sight of God" (Acts 8:21).

In Acts 13:6–12 Paul strikes with temporary blindness a man called Bar-jesus or Elymas. Paul wasted no words in telling him what he thought of him, ". . . O full of all subtilty and all mischief, you child of the devil, you enemy of all righteousness, will you not cease to pervert the right ways of the Lord?" (Acts 13:10).

The propagation of error is a sin that needs to be dealt with openly and promptly since it seeks to lead others astray. But personal sin must be dealt with as circumspectly as possible with every precaution being taken so that it does not become a scandal. Who knows how much harm has been done to the cause of Christ from loose and shameful gossip! Paul affirms that the case he is dealing with here is not a matter of gossip, but a fact of immoral conduct by a member of the Corinthian church.

Gossip Travels Fast

Paul does not say "generally we hear," or "I hear," but "commonly it is heard." He refers to the inevitability of the spreading of gossip. It travels with lightning speed.

The Sin Was Well-Publicized

No special effort was needed to hear what was going on. Evidently it was being talked about all over, for Paul had heard it even in Ephesus, and it seems that it may even have affected his own ministry. There would be those who would say to him, "Are these the people you evangelized? Are these the people who are 'sanctified in Christ Jesus, called to be saints' [1 Cor. 1:2]? Look what is going on in Corinth! They tolerate such fornication there as is not so much as even mentioned among the heathen people."

Such is the inevitable harm that comes as a result of sin in any part of the body of Christ. Paul was not only concerned about the evil of fornication within the Corinthian church, but he was alarmed that the news of it was being spread far and wide. He does not say, "I received word of the fornication which exists among you," but, "It is reported commonly that there is fornication among you."

The phrase "there is" does not appear in the Greek text. The verb *akoúetai* means "is heard" or "is reported" as the KJV has it. Paul admonishes, "That there is fornication in your midst is public knowledge; I wish it were not. Even if it were not known, I would still ask you to deal with it along with me. But since it is public knowledge, it is the responsibility of all of you to immediately take remedial measures."

The apostle Paul then candidly specifies the instance of fornication which they were tolerating: "And such fornication as is not so much as named among the Gentiles, that one should have his father's wife." He does not deem it necessary to name the person. Paul's main purpose is to uphold a principle of morality, to remedy the sin, not simply to condemn the sinner.

We Instinctively Know What Is Wrong

Why does Paul say, "and such fornication as is not so much as named among the Gentiles"? Is it because these two, son and stepmother, were Jews? The Jews had a law against such behavior, namely that prescribed in Leviticus 18:8 and Deuteronomy 22:30, but the Greeks did not; in fact, they did not even have a word to describe incest. Secular Roman law also forbade such union. Even the heathen had innate knowledge of the evil of incestual relations, so much so that the subject was unmentionable.

Is it any wonder that Paul wanted quick action in regard to this gross immorality in the Christian church in Corinth? This quick action is indicated in 2 Corinthians 7:12: "Wherefore, though I wrote unto you, I did it not for his cause that had done the wrong [the stepson who was committing incest], nor for his cause that suffered wrong [probably the father], but that our care for you in the sight of God might appear unto you." This is where Paul refers back to First Corinthians chapter five and the action he had recommended.

The Greek word translated "care" is *spoudḗn* (*spoudḗ*, nom.) from *speúdō* which means "to urge, press, hasten."[1] It should properly be translated "urgent care" or "diligent concern": "What urgent concern it [this incest] worked in you, yes, what clearing of yourselves, yes, what indignation, yes, what fear, yes, what vehement desire, yes, what zeal, yes, what revenge! In all things you have approved yourselves to be clear in this matter." Verse twelve should read: "Wherefore, though I wrote unto you, I did it not for his cause that had done the wrong, nor for his cause that suffered wrong, but that our urgent concern, our care for you in the sight of God, might appear unto you." Paul desired to show his sincere concern and urgent care for the Corinthian believers and their standing before God. The church and her testimony was Paul's immediate concern. His corrective action did not spring merely from a desire to punish the sinner and comfort the one who suffered the result of incest, namely the father, but rather from his zeal to preserve the testimony of the local church in Corinth and of the church universal.

1. *Spoudḗ* means "haste," as in Mark 6:25; 2 Pet. 1:5 and Jude 1:3 "diligence"; in 2 Cor. 8:8 "forwardness," and 2 Cor. 8:16, "earnest care." The only occurrences of the word where the translators of the KJV omitted the idea of urgency are in 2 Corinthians 7:11, 12 involving Paul's corrective concern about this case of incest in Corinth. In verse eleven *spoudḗi* is translated "carefulness" and in verse twelve, "care."

Upholding the Purity of the Church Is More Important than Protecting Personalities

Discipline in the Christian church, therefore, must always transcend personalities. It should uphold principles. Human law punishes the evildoer. It can hardly do more. Christians, however, must give first priority to upholding the purity of the church and assign a secondary role to the discipline of the erring individual. They must never give the world the impression that the church is tolerant of moral evil into which a member may fall.

Finally, is the question as to when the offending person had become a member of the Christian community in Corinth. We are not told, but it is safe to assume that it was before he fell into this sin. As soon as Paul heard of this breach of conduct, he acted. Perhaps the Corinthian church did not give immediate attention to this gross immorality because they were so taken up with party strife (1 Cor. 1:12–13) or with the exhibition of their presumed spiritual gifts (1 Cor. 12). Their personal pride and bickering may have been more important to them than the purity of the church or the restoration of a sinful brother. The church's first business is to its likeness to its Master.

There is absolutely no mention of the culpability of the stepmother in this sordid affair. Perhaps she was an unbeliever. Any judgment that the Corinthian church would pronounce on her would be irrelevant to the responsibility of the church to deal with her own members first. Even if she had lured her stepson to this sin of incest, it did not reduce the severity of the sin of the one who was related to the church. Sin by consent is just as reprehensible as that by the initiator.

Unmentionable Sin

The case in the Corinthian church involved a young man who was committing incest with his father's wife or his stepmother.

The text specifies his father's wife which in the Septuagint is the translation of *asat ab,* an Old Testament rabbinical term for stepmother.[2] However, the text does not mention the father which may indicate that he was either dead or divorced from his wife.

This incest Paul clearly calls *porneía*, or fornication, a general Greek term which includes adultery and incest as well as other sexual sins.

Scriptural Usages of the Word "Fornication"

Porneía, the substantive from *porneúō*, to commit fornication, has the following usages:

1) In general it denotes whoredom, that is intercourse between the sexes outside of lawful marriage (see also 2 Cor. 12:21; Eph. 5:3; Col. 3:5; 1 Thess. 4:3; cf. Acts 15:20, 29; 21:25; 1 Cor. 6:13, 18).

2) Fornication between two unmarried persons as distinguished from *moicheía*, "adultery," and *asélgeia*, "lasciviousness," insatiable lust of other kinds (Mark 7:21), and also from *akatharsía*, "uncleanness" (Gal. 5:19) caused by other sins.

3) Whoredom or adultery by a married woman (Matt. 5:32; 19:9).

4) Incestuous cohabitation (as here in 1 Cor. 5:1).

5) Every form of lewdness (Rom. 1:29). Paul often includes all kinds of uncleanness under the name of *porneía*, fornication (cf. 2 Cor. 12:21, Eph. 5:3; 1 Thess. 4:3; see also v. 7).

6) The participation of Christians in idolatrous worship which often was accompanied with prostitution (Rev. 2:21; 14:8; 17:2, 4; 18:3; 19:2) and which was a violation of the sym-

---

2.A parallel of this passage is found in Martial Epigrammata 4.16.

bolic marriage between Christ and His church. In this sense it is generally used in the Septuagint for physical fornication or whoredom (e.g., Gen. 38:24; Hos. 1:2).

The verb *porneúō*, "to commit fornication" which is derived from *pórnē*, "a female fornicator or harlot," has the following meanings:

1) To commit whoredom, to act as a whore (1 Cor. 6:18; 10:8; Rev. 2:14, 20).

2) To perpetrate spiritual whoredom against God or Christ by communication in idolatrous worship which was frequently accompanied, as in 1 Corinthians 10:8 and Revelation 2:14, 20, with bodily whoredom (Rev. 17:2–9).

Fornication Strictly Forbidden for Christians

Paul has taken it for granted that the Corinthian Christians knew that any sexual activity outside of legitimate marriage is sin. In 1 Corinthians 6:13 he writes: "The body is not for fornication [*porneía*], but for the Lord; and the Lord for the body." This implies that one cannot be the Lord's and at the same time commit fornication. It is actually here in 1 Corinthians 5:1, while speaking of this sexual relationship between a son and his stepmother, that Paul first mentions fornication. Whether his father, the husband of this woman, was alive or not seems irrelevant, for Paul does not mention it.

In Leviticus 18:8 it is clearly stated that not only is such a marriage forbidden, but that a son should not even be permitted to see his mother's nakedness: "The nakedness of thy father's wife you shall not uncover; it is your father's nakedness." Similarly and more explicitly is the statement in Deuteronomy 22:30: "A man shall not take his father's wife, nor discover his father's skirt."

Legality Is Not Necessarily Morality

At the time Paul wrote this epistle, Corinth was a Roman colony, and Roman law did not permit a son to marry his mother. We can conclude therefore that this incestual relationship was not consummated as an official marriage. But even if it had been sanctioned by the state or the laws of a country, it would still have been intrinsically immoral. Public sanction of wrongdoing does not make it right. If, for instance, the state should legalize marriage between couples of the same sex, that would not in the sight of God make homosexual "marriages" moral. One might thus be legally married but live in sin all his or her life. The government of men cannot change God's eternal and unalterable law. In our sexual relationships, we should not simply conform to the law of the state, but we must adhere to what God directs or permits. In the instance Paul is dealing with, both Roman law and God's law forbade a marriage between a son and his mother. And God's law went one step farther: it forbade not only a sexual relationship with or without marriage between a son and his mother, it even forbade a mother to expose her nakedness to her son. This whole sordid state of affairs in Corinth could have possibly begun in just that way: the mother may not have been as discreet as she should have been.

Mothers and fathers bear a tremendous responsibility before God to exhibit modest and honorable behavior before their sons and daughters. Let us remember what our Lord said about the eye becoming a trap unto fornication: "But I say unto you, that whosoever looks on a woman to lust after her has committed adultery with her already in his heart. And if your right eye offend you, pluck it out, and cast it from you: for it is profitable for you that one of your members should perish, and not that your whole body should be cast into hell" (Matt. 5:28, 29). It is wise for both a mother and a father to be careful what he or she exposes before the eyes of their children lest they are tempted, if not to actual fornication, to fornication in the heart which is equally condemned by our Savior. What a responsibility a parent has! The way parents dress or do not dress may spell the downfall of their own sons or daughters. What a shocking desire for a man or woman to want to be sexually appealing to his or her children!

Wealth and Knowledge—Temptations to Pride

The verb *phusióō*, "to puff up," is used only by Paul, primarily in his first letter to the Corinthians. It is fascinating to see the various contexts in which he uses the verb.

The Contrast between the Corinthians and the Apostles

In 1 Corinthians 4:6 Paul says, "And these things, brethren, I have in a figure transferred to myself and to Apollos for your sakes; that you might learn in us not to think of men above that which is written, that no one of you be puffed up [*phusioústhē*] for one against another." This entire fourth chapter is a contrast between the material affluence of the Corinthians and his own poverty and sacrifice for Christ.

In verse eight he writes: "Now you are full, now you are rich, you have reigned as kings without us: and I would to God you did reign, that we also might reign with you." They were people with a great deal of money and much knowledge.

In verse nine, Paul speaks about himself and the other apostles, "For I think that God has set forth the apostles last, as it were appointed to death: for we are made a spectacle unto the world, and to angels, and to men." He continues: "We are fools for Christ's sake, but you are wise in Christ; we are weak, but you are strong; you are honorable, but we are despised. Even unto this present hour we both hunger, and thirst, and are naked, and are buffeted, and have no certain dwelling place. And we labor, working with our own hands: being reviled, we bless; being persecuted, we suffer it: being defamed, we entreat: we are made as the filth of the world, and are the offscouring of all things unto this day."

It is in this context that Paul says in the last part of verse six, "That no one of you be puffed up for one against another." And then in verse eighteen he uses the word again: "Now some are puffed up [*ephusiōthēsan*] as though I would not come to you." Paul's conclusion is that material affluence blows up a person out of proportion and sets one against the other. Thus, where there are fights among Christians, frequently it is because some Christians have become puffed up because of their material possessions. We should beware of that affluence which exalts us and demeans our fellow believers who, though poor, may be God's chosen vessels who have given much for the service of their Lord.

In a certain pond there were two ducks and a frog. There was little rain, and the pond began to dry up. Both the ducks and the frog realized that they would soon have to vacate. The ducks could easily fly to another place, but what about their friend, the frog?

The frog came up with the suggestion that the ducks would hold a stick in their beaks and he would hang onto the stick with his mouth, and thus they would fly him to another pond. As they were flying overhead, a farmer who looked up and saw them said, "Well, isn't that a clever idea! I wonder who thought of it?" Bursting with pride, the frog could not contain himself and shouted to the farmer, "I did. . . ." What happened to the self-congratulating frog happens also to a proud person. His fall is inevitable.

In 1 Corinthians 8:1 the verb *phusióō* is used again: "Now as touching things offered unto idols, we know that we all have knowledge. Knowledge puffeth up [*phusioí*], but charity edifieth."

The word *gnō̃sis* is used in this verse for knowledge, which means acquired or experiential knowledge. The apostle is saying that the more one thinks he knows, the more he blows himself out of proportion. He prefers not to spend time building up others or edifying them.

The word for "edifieth" here is *oikodomeí*, from *oíkos*, "house," and *doméō*, "to build." It is used here in a spiritual sense of building the church of Christ (see also Matt. 16:18; 21:42; Mark 12:10; Luke 20:17; Acts 4:11; 1 Pet. 2:5, 7). Generally it means to profit spiritually as in 1 Corinthians 8:1; 14:4. Therefore, the verb *phusióō*, "to puff up," stands here as the opposite of *oikodoméō*, "to build up." Knowledge puffs up the individual, but love works to firmly establish others on a sound foundation. Knowledge seeks to understand things while love (*agápē*) seeks to help people grow. What Paul is trying to describe here is the highbrow, the man who is educated above his intelligence and brags about things in a language others cannot understand in order to make them look and feel inferior.

Years ago in North Carolina there was a poor farmer whose son was very bright. He and his wife decided that the boy deserved as good an education as anyone else, and they sacrificed a great deal to send him to college. He sent lovely letters of appreciation home. In time the father grew homesick for his son, so he loaded up his old farm wagon and started off to the college town. It was a long and tedious journey, but finally he arrived, and from a distance he thought he recognized his son.

"There he comes! There he comes!" said the old man. He jumped off the wagon and ran to meet his son, who had not yet seen him. "My son," he cried. The boy was surprised, but he was not glad. He was ashamed of his father in his faded old overalls before his two college companions.

"There must be some mistake, sir," he said. "I am not your son; you are not my father. I do not know you. There must be some mistake, sir!"

He might as well have driven a knife into his father's heart. The man went home with a broken heart. Knowledge had puffed up his son so much that love had left him.

It is not only ignorant people who may be proud, but also those who know the most. They are often so proud of what they know that they do not realize there is much more that they do not know.

Pride is a dangerous sin. It is like a building raised several stories higher than the strength of the foundation will allow. When it leads to a fall, the damage will be great indeed and may destroy others, too.

LESSONS:

1. Every action of the believer should be guided by the way it will affect someone else, and the way it will affect the cause of Christ.
2. When an individual in a Christian community does something wrong and it is publicized, even if the individual is restored, the stain on the Christian community remains.
3. Personal sin must be carefully dealt with so that it does not become a scandal, for the propagation of error seeks to lead many astray.
4. By not stating the name of the person involved in incestous sin, Paul shows that his main purpose is not to condemn the sinner, but to uphold a principle of morality and remedy the sin.
5. Christians should first uphold the purity of the church and in so doing, should discipline erring individuals, never tolerating the moral evil into which a member may fall.
6. Roman law forbade marriage between mother and son, whereas God's law forbade a mother to even expose her nakedness to her son.

1 Cor. 5:2 — *Pride Which Should Have Been Shame*

And ye are puffed up, and have not rather mourned, that he that hath done this deed might be taken away from among you.

The unconcerned attitude of the Corinthian believers regarding the publicized incest of one of their fellowship was of great concern to Paul, as it ought to have been. He wrote to them: "And [but] you are puffed up. . . ." The meaning of the verb *phusióō* or *phusiáō* is "to blow up" (*phusáō*). Figuratively it refers to being inflated with pride and vanity. It is used by Paul particularly in his Corinthian epistles. For instance, in 1 Corinthians 8:1 he makes a basic statement: "Knowledge puffs up." To these same Corinthians Paul wrote in 1 Corinthians 13:2: "Though I have . . . all knowledge . . . and have not love, I am nothing." They were more educated and wealthy and consequently thought they had more spiritual gifts than other believers (1 Cor. 12). Paul warned them that inflated egos often accompany impoverished spirits.

The apostle Paul had earlier accused the Corinthians of this egotistical practice and attitude. In 1 Corinthians 4:6 he wrote: "That you might learn in us not to think of men above that which is written, that no one of you be puffed up [{5448} *phusioústhē*] for one against another." The Greek word for "another" is *hetérou*, which means another qualitatively. One child of God may be more educated and wealthy than his fellow believers; that ought not to make him proud, but humble, knowing that God gave him more opportunities and consequently more responsibilities.

We should realize that none of us has any basis for pride when we consider the words of 1 Corinthians 4:7: "For who makes you to differ from another? And what have you that you have not received? Now if you did receive it, why do you glory, as if you had not received it?"

Sin is inevitable when a man's heart is possessed by his possessions. A lady once asked a minister whether she might not be fond of her dress or an ornament without also being proud. "Madam," he said, "when you see the fox's tail peeping out of the hole, you may be sure the fox is inside."

It was the Corinthians' pride that prevented their acknowledgment of serious sin within their ranks.

Calling Sin by Another Name

Is it possible for a Christian to fall into immorality? Unfortunately it is. And when sin attacks a Christian and enters the Christian church, let us not try to cover it up or camouflage it and call it by softer names. This is dangerous.

A distinguished minister once preached a sermon on sin. One of his church officers afterward came to him in his study and said to the minister, "Dr. Jones, we don't want you to talk so plainly as you do about sin because if our boys and girls hear you talking so much about sin they will more easily become sinners. Call it a mistake if you will, but do not speak so plainly about sin."

The minister took down a small bottle and showed it to him. It was a bottle of strychnine and was marked "poison." "I see," he said, "what you want me to do. You want me to change the label. Suppose I take off this label marked 'poison' and put on some mild label, such as 'essence of peppermint.' Don't you see what happens? The milder the label, the more dangerous the poison."

Pastors Must Discourage Factionalism

Pride is like a fever which glows forth with a rosy flush that appears to the casual observer to indicate unusually good health and well-being, but in reality is a disease doing its destructive work. It is ironic that in no other church in the apostolic era was there found such sin as in Corinth, and yet the Corinthians were the ones who boasted the most about their spiritual gifts. May we conclude, therefore, that one who is proud of his spiritual gifts is more likely to tolerate sin and less likely to feel the urgency of dealing with it? The church that elevates ministers to the same level as Christ is more than likely to become puffed up and to wink at immorality in the lives of its members. It is only natural when a local church is divided into parties that pride arises in the hearts of people, not only for themselves but also for their party and for the particular preacher whom they put on a pedestal.

The church that is divided into factions is a replica of the Corinthian church, a carnal church. A minister should observe the development of such factions and in his preaching concentrate on exalting Jesus Christ and His leadership. He should diagnose the basis of any factionalism that may arise, attack the causes rather than the symptoms, and seek its abolition.

The Proud Cease to Be Cautious as to Moral Dangers

The people of any church who are puffed up may be careless regarding their moral integrity. "Let him that thinks he stands take heed lest he fall," Paul warns in 1 Corinthians 10:12. Pride deprives the believer of concern for the moral dangers that exist around him. He no longer recognizes the ability of Satan to attack even the most mature. If Satan did not think Christ to be an unlikely target of his attacks, how can he think that we are not prime targets for his temptations? Saintliness and pride are poor companions on the pathway to spiritual growth.

Could we ever conceive of a pastor turning to the very people he led to Jesus Christ and saying to them, "You are proud; you are puffed up; you blow yourselves out of proportion"? Paul had the courage to do just this. But his admonitions came from having seen the real results of this prideful puffing up. By mentioning their pride, Paul, like a good doctor, tackles the cause of the disease and not merely the symptoms. If we look carefully at the troubles that churches have today, it will not be long before we find pride to be a contributing factor. If each one of us would stop to examine himself carefully, we would soon find that pride has contributed to whatever overt sin is in our lives.

Blowing Oneself Out of Proportion

The common blow-fish or puffer, a flabby-looking, tough and rubbery fish, can blow itself up to twice its normal size when approached by other fish. Although it appears large and intimidating to the other fish, in reality it has simply filled its stomach with air. A short time later, however, it will just as suddenly and noisily collapse. What a perfect illustration of these Christians to whom Paul is writing!

The verb *phusióō* means to blow oneself out of proportion. It expresses a person's desire to make himself and others believe that he is better than he is. That is exactly what the Corinthians were doing. Because they had riches and gifts which they thought were of the Spirit, they were blowing themselves up. They did not really want to look into the mirror of God's Word and see their true profile.

This subject reminds me of a story about Queen Elizabeth I. As she advanced in years, her wrinkles deepened. The master of the mint wanted to place an exact likeness of the queen on the coins and paper money, and so he reproduced her appearance, wrinkles and all. What did the queen do? Did she reward him for his perfection? No. She dismissed him because he produced a faithful likeness of her and ordered that the die be destroyed. Only one mutilated specimen of a shilling is now in existence showing Queen Elizabeth I as she appeared at that time.

The queen's maids, however, wishing to flatter her, removed all mirrors from the palace. A journalist at the time wrote: "The queen has not had the heart to look herself in the face for the last twenty years." The queen rewarded the maids for their attempt at flattery, while she punished the sincere and honest master of the mint.

Paul was like the master of the mint who revealed to the Corinthians their true condition. As ministers of the gospel, have we, like Paul, had the courage to look at our congregations and confess what they really are? Have we looked at the mirror of the Word of God and seen what we really are? Have we, like the queen's maids, removed the mirror of God's Word from among our people or do we keep it before them all the time so that all may see their true appearance before God?

Pride that Leads Astray

A wit once said, "He who knows it all has a lot to learn." In reality, though, knowledge is not bad in itself. In 1 Corinthians 12:8 Paul presents the second gift of the Spirit as "the word of knowledge."

Knowledge Can Be Good or Bad

In 1 Corinthians 13:2, however, Paul qualifies the effect that knowledge can have on an individual. "And though I have . . . all knowledge . . . and have not love, it profits me nothing." Knowledge, thus, can be of little value or of great value depending on the effect it has on the person who possesses it. If one's knowledge is interwoven with love so that it is used to build others up and not merely to blow oneself out of proportion, it can indeed be a gift of the Spirit of God, the result of grace (*chárisma*).

The trouble in Corinth was that God's gifts, one of which was knowledge, were being misused and misapplied. If we do not understand this, we shall have great difficulty in understanding First Corinthians chapters twelve through fourteen. In chapter twelve Paul speaks of the gifts of the Spirit, but then in chapter thirteen he speaks of love which is the instrument whereby these gifts may be properly utilized. Here he also speaks of the misuse of at least one gift, the ability which God gave at certain times to the Jews (Acts 2), to the Gentiles (Acts 10, 11), and to the disciples of John (Acts 19) to speak in languages they had not learned. This gift accompanied the baptism of the Holy Spirit by which these three groups of believers and all believers hereafter were incorporated into the body of Christ (1 Cor. 12:13). Therefore, 1 Corinthians 8:1, stating that "Knowledge puffs up," should be taken with 1 Corinthians 13:4 where Paul says, "Love . . . is not puffed up [*phusioútai*]."

Pride Produced by the Fleshly Mind

In Colossians 2:18 Paul once again uses this verb *phusióō*, "to puff up," and gives as its basis the fleshly mind: "vainly puffed up by his fleshly mind." Paul refers to the arbitrator between the Colossians and those Judaizers who opposed them by teaching that a Christian should keep the Law of Moses. The arbitrator was to judge who was right and who was wrong. He would arrive at a rash conclusion and judge vainly if he was proud and governed by the mind of his flesh.

Flesh, of course, stands here, as in many other parts of the New Testament, for carnality or the propensity of man to satisfy and please his sensual desires. The implication is that the sins of the flesh, of which *porneía*, "fornication," is one, begin with the perverted mind. This was definitely taught by our Lord in Matthew 5:27–31: adultery or fornication begins with the eye. It is conceived first in the mind, and then it is expressed overtly.

Pride Refuses to Restore a Repentant Sinner

Second Corinthians 2:1–10 apparently deals with the case of incest recorded in 1 Corinthians 5:1–5. When Paul says in verse six "Sufficient to such a man is this punishment, which was inflicted of many," he is apparently speaking of the young man who had committed incest with his stepmother. Apparently there were those in the Corinthian church who did not want to take the repentant member back into the fellowship of the Christian community, even after he had repenteded of his sin. Accordingly, Paul instructs them in verse seven, "So that contrariwise you ought rather to forgive him, and comfort him, lest perhaps such a one should be swallowed up with overmuch sorrow. . . ."

Second Corinthians 7:12 also should be connected with this incident: "Wherefore, though I wrote unto you, I did it not for his cause that had done the wrong [i.e., the man who had committed adultery or fornication with his stepmother]." But what did Paul mean when he further wrote, "nor for his cause that suffered wrong"? Here he refers to the innocent victims of the whole situation. Previously we stated our suspicion that this young man's father may have been dead, otherwise somehow he would have appeared on the scene. But if he were alive, he must have been greatly hurt as were any other relatives of the family. Although Paul's recommended action in this case purposed to have the incestuous young man disciplined, as he apparently was by the church, yet he wanted the Corinthian believers to realize his main concern was that he cared for them. Hence he continues, "but that our care for you in the sight of God might appear unto you." In other words, Paul's primary concern was neither for the injured family, nor for the son himself, but for the preservation of the purity of the local church.

Pride Was Second Nature to the Corinthians

It seems that Paul attributed all the evils that characterized the conduct of the Corinthians to their proud nature since he states so many times that they are proud or "puffed up." This word, *pephusiōménoi*, "you are puffed up," is a perfect passive participle, which means that they were in a state that had become second nature to them. The forms are the same for the perfect middle and passive voices, but here the meaning being middle, the voice must be taken as middle: "You have puffed up yourselves." These Corinthians had developed such an attitude of pride that they would not admit that anything they were doing was wrong. Although they permitted evil in the church, the Corinthians denied that their church was inferior to others. A proud person will not only commit sin, but he will try to hide it. And if it should come out into the open, he will try to justify or excuse it, attributing it to the weakness of the flesh and pointing out that we are all thus subject to sin. The Corinthians might well have blamed the evil environment in which they lived for the downfall of this young man, and so they tolerated it. It is against such toleration that Paul is most incensed.

The Perfect Rebuke to Pride

All of us ought to ask God to "pour contempt on all our pride." The life and death of our Lord Jesus Christ stand as a rebuke to every form of pride to which men are prone:

Pride of birth and rank: "Is not this the carpenter's son?" (Mark 6:3).

Pride of wealth: "The Son of Man has not where to lay His head" (Matt. 8:20).

Pride of personal appearance: "He has no form nor comeliness" (Is. 53:2).

Pride of reputation: "A friend of publicans and sinners!" (Matt. 11:19; Luke 7:34).

Pride of learning: "How knows this man letters, having never learned?" (John 7:15).

Pride of superiority: "I am among you as he that serves" (Luke 22:27).

Pride of success: "He came unto his own, and his own received him not" (John 1:11). "Neither did his brethren believe on him" (John 7:5). "He was despised and rejected of men" (Is. 53:3).

Pride of ability: "I can of my own self do nothing" (John 5:30).

Pride of self-will: "I seek not my own will, but the will of Him that sent me" (John 5:30).

Pride of intellect: "As my Father has taught me, I speak these things" (John 8:28).

Pride in death: "He became obedient unto death, even the death of the cross" (Phil. 2:8).

Let us examine ourselves. Are we following the example of our Lord?

Uniformly, the ambassadors and rulers of small nations are resplendent in gold braid and glittering uniforms, but the representatives and monarchs of the great nations are distinguished by their less assuming attire. Just what appearance do we attempt to exhibit?

Tolerating Sin in the Christian Church

To remain indifferent in the midst of an urgent, morally unhealthy situation is inexcusable for Christians. Action is necessary on an individual and a corporate basis. Inaction is simply intolerable.

The Need for Concern

The apostle Paul was deeply concerned when he learned of the widespread publicity surrounding the case of incest of a son with his stepmother and the church's lack of response. This young man, from all indications, was part of the Christian congregation of Corinth while his stepmother may not have been. This may be surmised from the fact that only he is singled out for discipline while his stepmother is not mentioned at all.

Perhaps we may learn from this that the concern of the Christian church should be primarily focused upon the lives of its members or communicants and secondarily upon the affairs of the world. After all, the internal church situation may be effectively corrected, whereas the external situation can only be influenced to a limited degree. The similarity between the family of God and an earthly family is very close. Is not the parents' first responsibility to their own children or that of one family member to another family member? This analogy usually proves true.

Unconverted People May Penetrate the Church

Another conclusion arising from this situation is that it is possible for a person to infiltrate the local community of believers without being truly saved. We as human guardians of Christ's church can be mistaken in our judgment of the genuineness of one's profession of faith. The whole congregation must not be branded as immoral and inconsistent because one or more of its members or those attached to a local church fall into grievous sin. It can happen to any congregation; therefore, let not any congregation boast of its total integrity. Any purity in the lives of the communicants of a local Christian congregation is due to the grace of God. Thus, in reality, no church should condemn another because of the behavior of some of its members.

The Church Did Not Act Immediately

In 1 Corinthians 5:2 Paul says, "And ye are puffed up, and have not rather mourned, that he that hath done this deed might be taken away from among you." The first word is the conjunction *kaí*, "and," which in this instance has the strength of an adversative instead of a connective.; it could be rendered "but." In spite of the publicity of this sin, Paul stresses that the church had not yet responded appropriately.

Rather than write to the elders of the church at Corinth or to its pastor or teacher who must have succeeded him in this local ministry, Paul writes to all of the church. He says *humeís*, "you," implying all of them. Every member must share the responsibility. What another does may be beyond our personal control, but when it concerns the household of faith of which we are a part, it becomes our responsibility to act resolutely and promptly. It is improper for a lay person to shrug his or her shoulders and to shirk that responsibility in the face of a situation in need of correction. When one member suffers, all must suffer. That is the clear teaching of Paul in 1 Corinthians 12:14–27. We must never say, "Let the pastor or the elders take care of the situation." It is just as much the responsibility of a church member as it is for one who holds an office in the church.

No Synodical Church Intervention, but Personal, Fatherly Concern

Paul does not send a delegation of church dignitaries from other cities to solve the Corinthian situation. The apostle already had established congregations in Philippi, Thessalonica, Berea, and possibly Athens on his second missionary journey, but he does not involve the leaders of those churches in the solution of the Corinthian problem. Synodical or denominational external jurisdiction upon a local church from delegates of other churches does not seem to be the prescribed apostolic pattern. This passage rather implies the autonomy of the local congregation.

Paul nevertheless showed personal concern, even though as an apostle he was not one of the original twelve who had followed the life of Christ and thus had unique apostolic authority. His concern was principally due to his personal attachment to the church of Corinth, since he was the first one to preach the gospel there and he labored among the Corinthians for a year and a half. They were his children in the faith; he was their spiritual father.

Paul did not assert his apostolic authority and force it upon the local church. In the entire New Testament, we hardly find any apostle who imposed his solutions in an authoritarian manner in the matter of local church disciplinary problems. The apostles' basic concern was that inadequate or erroneous local doctrinal teaching should not penetrate the church.

Apostolic Delegations Sent to Correct Doctrinal Error

Consider the situation in Samaria as described in Acts 8. Philip the deacon was preaching there. He attracted many, not only with his preaching but also with "the signs and wonders" which he worked among them. Philip, however, deceived as to the genuineness of the profession of faith of a sorcerer by the name of Simon, baptized him. The baptism was only in the name of the Lord Jesus without the inward grace of the Holy Spirit, without which any water baptism is invalid. The Holy Spirit is the element whereby Christ attaches the believers to His body (1 Cor. 12:13). Having heard about the spurious water baptisms in Samaria, the apostles in Jerusalem sent Peter and John to pray for these new believers in order that they might receive the Holy Spirit and thus be truly attached to Christ's body. This was not a matter of policy of a local church, but a doctrinal matter of great importance—the doctrine of the work of the Holy Spirit.

The next assemblage of apostles we find is in Jerusalem as described in Acts 15. Again, this was not for the purpose of settling a disciplinary matter of a local church, but for determining whether new believers in Christ should be circumcised and keep the Law of Moses (v. 5). Here we have participation by the apostles and elders (v. 6).

In both of these instances, fidelity to the Word of God and Christian doctrine itself was at stake. It seems that Paul did not advocate interference in local church policy by outsiders, but encouraged accountability to God by each individual church.

There is an autonomy about a local church which Paul respects and encourages when he invites the Corinthian church to gather together and act in the name of the Lord Jesus Christ in concordance with his own spirit. He did not issue a decree, but he asked the church to act, honoring Christ and respecting his apostolic advice.

Becoming Insensitive to Sin

In a certain village in Scotland lived a half-witted man whose coat presented a curious appearance. Down the front it was covered with patches of various sizes, mostly large. When asked why the coat was patched in such an unusual manner, he answered that the patches represented the sins of his neighbors. He pointed to each patch and gave the story of the sin of someone in the village, then went on to another and another until he had related the sins of all in the village. On the back of his coat there was a little patch no bigger than a small coin. On being asked what that one represented, he said, “That’s my own sin, and I cannot see it!”

That is the kind of coat the Corinthians usually wore. As one reads Second Corinthians chapter eight where Paul compares these southern Greeks with the Macedonian or northern Greeks, he will come to realize this is so. The Macedonians were poor, but they were generous. The Corinthians were generous also, but their generosity, since they were affluent, did not represent a sacrifice on their part. They were so proud, however, that they could not see the superiority of the gifts of the Macedonian churches. What a great pity when an individual or a church becomes insensitive to sin and its consequences.

In 1983, a Korean airliner with 269 people aboard strayed into Russian airspace and was shot down killing all on board. No one knows whether or not the pilot knew that he had strayed off the prescribed route. Deviation from the prescribed course, whether inadvertently or purposefully, can be disastrous.

This is what happened to the Corinthians as they tolerated a young man who had strayed morally. Sexual sin was so prevalent in Corinth that even in the Corinthian church situational ethics were accepted.

One of the most destructive effects of television is the introduction of the subtle acceptability of sin as the normal course of life. As one sees sin perpetrated and fully accepted in front of his own eyes and in his own home day after day, he tends to lose his sensitivity to it. Violence and immorality have come into our living rooms and consequently have produced violent and immoral people. TV has desensitized even those with high standards. The same impact was made on the Corinthian Christians since the pagan temple was the center of activity. An example of this impact was that the official temple prostitutes were called priestesses or *hierodouloi*, "the slaves of the holy."

Our Inner Attitude and the Environment

Yielding to sin depends not on the surrounding circumstances but on the inner conviction of the heart. Joseph, while enslaved in a foreign land, was the object of the immoral temptations of his master's wife, and yet he resisted. But in Corinth a young man living in his own home could not resist the sexual impulse he had with his own stepmother. One can never blame the environment for his own sinful propensity.

Perhaps the reason the Corinthians overlooked the sin of this young man was to excuse themselves for their own fornication. No wonder Paul said to them in 1 Corinthians 6:18, "Flee fornication."

In Cleveland, Ohio a misguided minister said in a sermon, "There is no meaning or value in condemning sex offenders as criminals, moral offenders, or social pariahs, anymore than there would be in criticizing or punishing a tubercular or a cripple. What is a sex offender but an emotional cripple?"

No doubt some in the Corinthian church had the same attitude about this young man. But Paul wanted to impress upon them that failure to deal realistically with sin and man's need to repent from it leads to the ruin of individuals and ultimately the downfall of a church or a nation. Unregenerate evildoers will continue in their dark, downward way until transformed by divine grace. "The heart of the sons of men is fully set in them to do evil" (Eccl. 8:11).

The Hidden Hook of Sin

The apostle Paul endeavored to deal promptly with the problem in Corinth lest sin should get a foothold in the Christian church.

Sin can be compared to the little worm at the end of the fishing line. As the fish swims by, he sees the tempting little morsel just waiting there for him. What is there to hinder his enjoyment of it? One little snap and down goes the worm and off swims the fish smug and satisfied—for a while! But that worm has a hook in it which is attached to a line and the fish can only swim away so far before the hook is set. Then, all too often, the more the fish struggles to get free, the tighter the hook sets. The poor fish had no idea that the tasty little morsel he enjoyed for such a short time was actually controlled by a set of hands in a world he didn't even know existed!

Temptations to sin may be small; they may be enticing, and no one may know about them. However, there is a hook hidden inside; the line is limited and controlled by something far beyond one's comprehension, but once the hook is set, the chances of getting free again are limited. Satan, the enemy of souls, is too shrewd to ask a man to descend precipitously into the depths of sin. His method is to lure a man on, one step at a time, finally bringing him to the point of no return where he is bound body and soul.

This was the situation that Paul was afraid was developing in Corinth and, sad to say, has developed in many instances in the modern, twentieth century church. Satan has lured many of God's children to accept less than the best He has planned for them—a holy and untainted walk with their Master.

Mourning Over Sin

The proper attitude to have when dealing with sin in the church of Corinth should have been to mourn over it. Paul said to the Corinthians, ". . . Ye are puffed up and have not rather mourned."

Mourning—a Characteristic of the Regenerate Heart

The word "mourn" in Greek is *penthéō*, from *pénthos*. It means to mourn, to grieve upon the death of a friend or loved one (see also Mark 16:10; James 4:9). In 2 Corinthians 12:21 it is used transitively meaning to bewail or mourn over or for. The substantive *pénthos* etymologically is deduced from *páthos*, "suffering," therefore meaning to mourn or sorrow or express grief, as is also found in Revelation 18:7, 8; 21:4. It is the expression of feeling that one has as he looks upon a friend or a loved one who has died.

The first time the verb is used in the New Testament is in the second Beatitude in Matthew 5:4: "Blessed are they that mourn for they shall be comforted."

The first Beatitude concerns the ones who recognize their spiritual helplessness (*ptōchoí tṓ pnéumati*). This is the basic condition which makes a man seek Christ. It is like someone who is drowning in the water. As long as he believes that he can save himself, he will not call for help. If he is too proud to recognize his helplessness, he will never be saved. The first step, therefore, to blessedness, God's indwelling the human heart as a result of calling upon Jesus Christ (Matt. 5:11), is the recognition of one's helplessness.

In the second Beatitude we have the first and immediate manifestation of the blessed person, the person who is indwelt by God and in whom He brings full and complete satisfaction. A sense of sorrow emerges immediately, a sense of mourning over his past sinful condition and over the sinful conditions existing around him. It is interesting that Paul diagnoses the basis of this deplorable sinfulness in Corinth as the pride of the Corinthians. He said to them accordingly, "You are puffed up"; and immediately he adds, "and you have not rather mourned." Pride does not allow a person to grieve for his sin or for the sins of others, yet Christ told us in the Beatitudes that mourning ought to be the first characteristic of the regenerated heart.

It Takes Humility to Mourn over Sin

The verb "mourn," is also given as a demand of Christians in James 4:9: "Be afflicted, and mourn, and weep." In order to understand why James gives this commandment, we must read verse six: "But he gives more grace. Wherefore he says, God resists the proud, but gives grace unto the humble." Mourning over sin is a characteristic of humility, and the absence of it is a characteristic of spiritual pride.

There is a pathetic story of Origen, a church father of antiquity, who had fallen into great backsliding. After a period of time, he began to turn back to the Lord again, and coming into a congregation, desired to preach. He opened the Bible randomly at the fiftieth psalm and began to read these words in the sixteenth and seventeenth verses: "But unto the wicked, God says, what have you to do to declare my statutes, or that you shouldest take my covenant in your mouth? Seeing you hate instruction, and cast my words behind you." Upon reading the words, Origen remembered his own backsliding and coming under great conviction he started to weep. He wept so bitterly that all the congregation was moved to weep with him. There is no doubt that preachers may be able to accomplish far more for their Lord by humbling themselves and confessing their shortcomings rather than by proudly declaring the truth while hiding their own sin.

There Should Be a Timely Reaction to Sin

The verb *epenthēsate* for "mourn" in this verse is in the second person plural first aorist indicative. The aorist tense suggests that the Corinthians should have mourned over this incident when it was first known to them. It refers to a particular time in the past when mourning should have been initiated and not ended until the situation was remedied. Action should have taken place at the proper time when this sin in their midst first became known.

One of the most unfortunate things in our society today is the delay of punishment of the criminal. Of course, rash or unfair punishment is not to be advocated, but just and speedy punishment would serve the interests of law and order. Even as evil should be nipped in the bud before it becomes a habit which is difficult to eradicate, so also crime should be contained by bringing the criminal to justice without undue delay. We have emphasized the necessity of being certain that no one is punished unjustly, but in so doing we have tolerated undue slowness in bringing the criminal to a speedy encounter with justice and due punishment.

The name given to the Greek mythological goddess of just vengeance was Nemesis. It was her duty to follow and punish the guilty. She had wings, but generally went on foot. This signified that the punishment of crime, although sure, is generally slow. An ancient poet says:

> Vengeance divine to punish sin moves slow.
> The slower its pace, the surer its blow.

In His goodness God delays punishment to give us the opportunity to repent. He has placed an immediate punishment, however, when one violates many of His physical laws. If one throws himself from a twenty-story window, he will be killed immediately, but if a person disobeys one of God's spiritual laws, the punishment may very likely be delayed. A good illustration of this is found in the disease of diabetes. A doctor explained to me that whenever a diabetic cheats on his diet which should be strictly regulated, certain but imperceptible damage is being done to the organs of his body. The results of violating the prescribed diet are usually not noticeable for many years, but each time the diabetic indulges in forbidden food, the deterioration of the body increases a little more. Eventually it may bring him to his deathbed.

Man takes advantage of God's longsuffering. The uncertainty of being caught and punished for a deed may well embolden a person to commit a sin. Although the young man in Corinth was living in incest, he probably was accepted in good standing in the Corinthian church. Such a situation would bring havoc to the very structure of the body of Christ. Persistent sin makes more difficult the recovery of the full usefulness of a church's witness.

The wisdom incorporated in the words of Ecclesiastes 8:11 cannot be disputed, "Because sentence against an evil work is not executed speedily, therefore the heart of the sons of men is fully set in them to do evil."

Paul tells the Corinthians that there should have been a time when, upon finding out about the sin of this young man, they should have dealt with it in all seriousness. Observe that he does not speak only of the grief that should have come into the heart of the sinner, but of that which should have affected all of them. Paul realizes the fundamental human trait that the sinner will not easily recognize his own sinfulness and voluntarily sever his church relationship.

The apostle addresses all the Corinthians, "You [pl.] are proud and you did not mourn." Why should they mourn? They were not the ones who had sinned. Nevertheless, the sin of one fellow worshiper ought to have affected all of them. As Paul said in 1 Corinthians 12:26 when speaking of the members of the body affecting one another and being concerned for one another, "And whether one member suffer, all the members suffer with it; or one member be honored, all the members rejoice with it." Had these hard-hearted Corinthians any real love for this fallen member of their group, they would have grieved or mourned as they besought the Lord for the restoration of their brother.

Dealing with Sin in the Church

Although mourning is a somewhat passive state, it emerges into action even as we see in the progression from the second Beatitude, "Blessed are they that mourn" (Matt. 5:4), to the third Beatitude. The immediate result of the indwelling of God within the human heart in giving the state of blessedness is the passive sorrow over sin, but then immediately follows the third Beatitude which says, "Blessed are the meek," meekness being a state wherein we are angry for a righteous reason, at the right person, at the right time, and for the right length of time.

Paul is very explicit about the action to which such mourning should have led the Corinthian church and reprimands them accordingly. The verb "mourned," which Paul used, is followed in Greek by the clause beginning with *hina*, which indicates "so that." The Greek text is actually far more harsh than the English translation would imply. A more accurate translation would have been, "so that he who did such a work be cast out from your midst." Sorrow over sin by itself does not accomplish much; it must lead to definitive and positive action. To mourn over the existence of sin in a church, a family, or a nation is not enough. The child of God must neither condone nor tolerate it, but resist it in God-given wisdom.

Excommunication of a Sinner from the Local Church

Certainly Paul does not suggest the toleration of the evildoer within the Christian community, but rather the casting out of such a one. Is this in conformity with the great love chapter which Paul writes in 1 Corinthians 13? Of course it is. In giving the characteristics of love, the apostle says that the first positive characteristic of love is that it suffers long (v. 4). That Greek word is *makrothumeí*, a word that applies only to individuals and not to situations or things. Another word, *hupoménei*, "to bear under or to be patient," is the appropriate word for toleration of adversity. Love seeks to redeem the sinner, but it cannot be tolerant and patient with the sin. This is exactly what Paul is advocating, and indeed it was successful because we find that this young man abandoned his sin and was reclaimed.

In 2 Corinthians 2:8 Paul admonished all the congregation "Wherefore I beseech you that you would confirm your love toward him." Thus casting out a sinner from a congregation, not simply to punish him but to redeem him and prevent the corruption of the whole body, is an act of love toward the person himself and toward the church of Christ. Punishment is not incongruous with the demonstration of Christian love. Loving a sinner does not involve permitting him to do whatever he wants—to overlook his sin. Is it not in this manner also with our own children? The goal in both cases is to lead him to realize that his sin is destructive to himself and to his community. He should be urged to forsake it, and assured that if he does so, he would be welcomed into the community of believers. The proud attitude of the Corinthians was evident even after this young man repented and came back to the local congregation. Apparently they had difficulty accepting their repentant brother into fellowship again.

Loving Expulsion

Paul uses the verb *exarthḗ*[1] to show the action that should have been taken against this man. These are the only two instances in the New Testament where this verb is used. In its basic sense the verb means "to lift up" or "to lift off of the earth." A more violent way of expressing this casting out would have been with the verbs *apobállō* or *ekbállō*, "to cast or throw out." There is a kind of gentleness to the verb *exaírō*. It indicates lifting up and then putting out, as if it were done tenderly, in order not to injure the person.

Thus, if we combine the verb "you did not mourn" with the verb "might be taken away," we see the attitude that the Corinthians were to have in this whole disciplinary action. They were not to cast this man out as a despised person, rejoicing in their hearts that they had separated him from their midst;

---

1. Third person singular first aorist subjunctive passive of *exaírō,* from *ex,* "out," and *aírō* "to take, remove."

rather, they were to weep over this situation. They were to look upon his removal with regret as if they were bearing a certain responsibility for his downfall.

There are two ways of putting out a brother who has sinned. He can be cast out as if there were no hope that he would ever return, or he can be lifted up and put out with tearful eyes and a broken heart that expects the grace of God to work even in the sinner's heart despite the repugnance of his sin. Love should not overlook sin; it should not compromise truth. When it is necessary to punish someone, it must be done in love. Correction is Christlike only when it is redemptive correction. Disciplining a child may be necessary, but how it is done may seriously affect the child's future development.

A sincere Christian elderly woman once said, "I have two daughters who take turns cleaning my little house. Jean comes and leaves everything shining, but she makes me feel I'm a heavy burden to her. But when Mary comes, no matter how dull the day or how low in spirit I am, she is so cheery and makes me feel she loves to be with me. They are both fine Christian women, but there is a great difference between the two."

Pallbearers and Stretcher Carriers

There are two kinds of people who carry out a sick person. There are the pallbearers who carry the sick out to bury him, never expecting him to be resurrected. Then there are the stretcher carriers who carry out the sick person for treatment, fully expecting that he will recover. The latter is what the Paul expects Christians to be when it is necessary for them to carry out an erring brother.

Removing Defilement

The apostle Paul never spoke of the young man who had fallen into the sin of fornication as though he were without hope. In fact, although this individual was committing fornication, Paul did not call him *pórnos*, a "fornicator." He simply said, "that he that has done this deed might be taken away from among you." Paul referred to his sin as if it were but one act or performance. The Greek word *érgon*, "work," indicates a single act or performance. Thus, the word is used here to denote a single evil act.

We cannot know exactly what the relationship was between this young man and his stepmother. In the previous verse Paul said, "That one should have his father's wife. . . ." The present infinitive *échein* describes the man's action as continuing, while the word *érgon*, "deed," denotes a single act. The verb *poiḗsas*, "he that hath done," is in the aorist tense which implies that he had committed the sin in the past as a completed act. If this were continuing, the apostle Paul would have used *poiṓn*, the present participle, instead of the aorist participle. We may reasonably deduce, then, that for a period of time this young man lived with his stepmother in an immoral sexual relationship. He did not officially marry her, having divorced her from her husband, his own father, if we assume that his stepmother was not a widow.

The Intolerable Effect of Incest

It is interesting that Paul does not use the verb *práxis* (*práttō*) as he usually does to indicate this evil act. *Poiéō*, which is used in this verse, usually denotes good deeds and not bad ones. A further point of interest is that *poiéō* indicates more the purpose or end of an act than the means by which this end is achieved. The latter is indicated more precisely by the verb *práttō* or *prássō*. In this connection we should note that three Alexandrian manuscripts do not use *poiḗsas* but *práxas*, probably because the copyists recognized that the verb *práttō* often conveys an unfavorable moral connotation (see John 3:20, 21; 5:29, etc.). We prefer *poiḗsas*. Paul wanted to point out that this young man, by his long-term sinful practice, had produced an evil effect, an end that was intolerable. Personalities are not to be considered at all when it comes to sinfulness within the Christian church. Sin does not become more or less tolerable because of the person or persons who commit it. It is the result of the sin that produces an effect upon the Christian church and causes her to be ineffective in her testimony as the light of the world. Paul is more concerned here about the practice of *porneía*, the acceptance of fornication, developing in the church as a result of the sinfulness of this young man, than about the particular sin as affecting one individual although that could in no way be ignored. A believer's sin is indeed deplorable, but its effect upon the Christian congregation where he or she worships is even more so. The putting away of such a sinner was important, but putting an end to the result of his sinfulness, the stigma and shame that had come upon the church, was imperative.

In verse two the aorist subjunctive passive of *exaírō* (*exarthḗ*), "that he may be removed," is used, and in verse thirteen the same verb is used for the second time in this chapter. It is *exareíte*,[2] "you will remove," which is the future active form indicating that this removal should be done at a definite time in the future by the Corinthians themselves. But why does Paul then admonish them in verse two, "that he be taken away," in the passive singular, and then in verse thirteen he says "put away" meaning that the Corinthians should do the removing? In verse two Paul indicates that such a person ought to be removed from the midst of the believers. This involves the necessity of such a removal by God and in consequence imposes a duty on the Christians of the Corinthian church to do the same. God ordains that discipline

2. Second person plural future indicative active of *exaírō*. The UBS text has it *exárate* which is the imperative of the first aorist in the second plural which for all practical purposes means the same.

be exercised in such cases, and He will see to it that the offender is removed. But it is also their duty, Paul stresses in verse thirteen, to do it themselves as instruments in the divine hands. Verse two implies that it is necessary to be done and verse thirteen urges that it be done by them since it is imperative.

Expelled from the Congregation, Not from the Kingdom of God

Paul does not suggest that such a person is cast out of the kingdom of God, if he were saved, or that he had lost his salvation, but that he should be cast out from among the Corinthian believers. Paul was sure this man would come back, repent of his sins, and be restored to the congregation, as seems to be the case in 2 Corinthians 2:6, 7: "Sufficient to such a man is this punishment, which was inflicted of many. So that contrariwise you ought rather to forgive him, and comfort him, lest perhaps such a one should be swallowed up with over much sorrow." Thus we conclude that a person who sins should be put away or separated from the local congregation not only because of the evil influence that results from such sinfulness, but also that such a person through this very excommunication may be rescued from his sin and restored to the fellowship of the Lord and of the local church. We do not find that this person made another profession of faith, but having repented of his sin, he was restored to the fellowship of believers. We may conclude, therefore, that it is likely that he was a believer who had fallen into sin (1 John 2:1).

We may infer from this incident that even if a person falls into fornication, he does not necessarily lose his salvation. A seeming contradiction is found in 1 Corinthians 6:9, 10 where we read, ". . . Be not deceived: neither fornicators, nor idolaters, nor adulterers, nor effeminate, nor abusers of themselves with mankind . . . shall inherit the kingdom of God." Revelation 22:15 likewise tells us that ". . . without are dogs, and sorcerers, and whoremongers, and murderers, and idolaters, and whosoever loveth and maketh a lie." However, these verses refer to people who practiced these evils as a way of life and not those who had fallen into such sin and recovered from it.

The Old Testament prescribes the action that should be followed in the case of fornication: "The hands of the witnesses shall be first upon him to put him to death, and afterward the hands of all the people. So you shall put the evil away from among you . . . and you shall put away the evil from Israel" (Deut. 17:7, 12; see also 22:21; 24:7). The Septuagint in all these verses uses the same verb *exareís*, "You shall take away." The word of God clearly teaches that a fornicator, as long as he continues in a lifestyle which is immoral, should be cast out of the fellowship of God's people.

Lessons:

1. Paul tackles the disease of the Corinthians, not merely its symptoms, when he tells of their pride.
2. Frequently the fights among Christians occur because some Christians have become puffed up by their material possessions.
3. Proud people are not always ignorant people; in fact, those who know the most are often so proud of what they know that they cannot see that there is much more they do not know.
4. Paul's primary concern was the purity of the local church.
5. Sorrow over sin alone does not accomplish much; it must lead to definitive and positive action.
6. The Corinthians were to weep over the removal of the incestuous young man with regret as if they were bearing a certain responsibility for his downfall.

1 Cor. 5:3, 4 | *Paul's Authority and Its Source*

For I verily, as absent in body, but present in spirit, have judged already, as though I were present, concerning him that hath so done this deed, In the name of our Lord Jesus Christ, when ye are gathered together, and my spirit, with the power of our Lord Jesus Christ, . . .

Paul distinguished himself from the local Christian church in Corinth for, although he established the church, he does not claim to be its leader. In his heart he cannot remain indifferent to what the Corinthians should do, but he wants them to take the initiative in the exercise of necessary discipline. The apostle makes no judgment, since there is really no apostolic enforcement of discipline within the local church. That discipline must come about by the local congregation itself.

Paul begins this verse with the emphatic "I" (*egṓ*). He does not contrast his position with the position of the church, for if he did, then he would have used not only the particle *mén*, but he would have followed it with the corresponding particle *dé*. In such a case he would have meant, "I, on the one hand [*mén*], make this judgment, and you, on the other hand [*dé*], should make this judgment." The conjunction *mén* used singularly here has more or less the meaning of "indeed" or "truly." Thus, the first three words of verse three should be translated "Therefore [*gár*], I [*egṓ*] truly [*mén*]," followed by the verb *kékrika*,[1] "have judged," that is, sometime in the past I made a judgment, and I am now of the same opinion. The perfect tense of the Greek word emphasizes not so much the act of the past as its present effect. Here Paul emphasizes his present opinion which was formed in the past as a proper judgment or determination.[2] He says, "I have decided [or determined]." This implies a fixed resolution or determination after having considered all aspects of the matter.

The first object of this verb (in reality there are two) concerns the young man who had committed fornication. This direct object is confused in the KJV by its insertion of the word "concerning" which does not occur in the Greek text. The Greek text does not say, "I have judged already concerning him that has so done this deed," but "I have judged him who perpetrated this deed in this manner." Paul had formed an opinion about this young man and had judged him in his own conscience and heart. He did not vacillate as to what should happen to this man, but was firm in his conviction.

It is apparent that this young man was not presently continuing this incestuous relationship. If he had been, the present participle, *tón katergazómenon* would have been used.[3] *Tón katergasámenon* definitely places this relationship in the past

---

1.First person singular perfect indicative active of *krínō,* "have judged."

2.See also Acts 15:19; 16:4; 20:16; 21:25; 25:5, etc.

3.The object of the verb "I have judged" is given as the participial substantive *tón,* "the," *katergasámenon,* in the aorist tense, indicating the one who in the past performed or perpetrated such a deed. The participial substantive *katergasámenon* is made up of the intensive *katá* and *ergázomai,* "to work," akin to *érgon,* "deed," of the previous verse. This compound verb is also used in Rom. 1:27; 2:9; 7:15, 17, 18 and Eph. 6:13.

and not as something that was occurring at the time Paul was writing. The use of the perfect tense *kékrika*, "have judged," indicates that the sinful deed, even if not of the present, must be dealt with. This young man could not say, "But I'm not doing it now." Nor could the Corinthian church merely put this sin behind them and refuse to deal with it. Every sin, whether of the past or the present, must be adequately dealt with. Sweeping it under the rug is not the answer either for the sinful individual or for the local church. God ultimately is going to bring up for judgment every unconfessed sin of the believer. The only way to avoid final judgment is to repent, confess, and abstain from all sin of the past, present and future.

Paul's Judgment Resulted from Personal Knowledge of the Situation

To confirm that he knew what he was doing, Paul qualifies himself as "being present." In other words, the apostle Paul is saying to these Corinthians, "Don't think that I have made this decision on heresay information. I know what has been going on as if I were present there, having personally followed the situation." This qualification he gives in the first part of the verse: "as absent in body, but yet present in spirit." It would have made no difference if the apostle Paul had been physically present with them; what he knew about the situation was nonetheless factual. It was through his spirit that he had made this judgment and not through the faculty of his body. A good example of this is that of a judge who does not need to go to the scene of the case that he tries; instead, he has all the evidence presented to him.

The second object of *kékrika*, the principal verb translated, "I have judged," is the infinitive *paradoúnai*, "to deliver," with which verse five begins. "I have judged," Paul says, "the man who perpetrated this, and my judgment is that he should be delivered to Satan."[4] The subject of "to deliver" is given once again. This time instead of saying "the one who perpetrated this in this manner" as in verse three, we have simply "such a one," referring, of course, to the one who had committed fornication. Every one belonging to that group should gather together, discuss the matter, and come to a decision. It was not a matter that should be kept only for the leadership of the church, but it should be of concern to the entire congregation. This is implied by the participle *sunachthéntōn.*[5] It means "those having come together": "You and my spirit having been come together." *Sunágō*, to "bring or come together," is the word from which "synagogue" is derived. The verb is in the aorist passive meaning that they would have come, been called or gathered together at a particular time for this very purpose. Apparently one meeting was enough to make the determination concerning this man. Paul wanted them to know that he bore the burden with them: "In the name of our Lord Jesus Christ . . . and my spirit, with the power of our Lord Jesus Christ." "Power" here is tantamount to enablement. It was a serious matter which they could not decide on their own. They needed to be fully dependent upon the power and enablement of the Lord Jesus Christ.

In a local congregation the pastor should take the same kind of leadership that the apostle Paul took, but he should not, on his own, or even in consultation with the other elders of the local body of believers, make a decision of this caliber. The decision must be made by the entire local congregation.

---

4. The infinitive "to deliver" is *paradoúnai,* the second aorist infinitive active of *paradídōmi,* from *pará,* denoting transition, and *dídōmi,* "to give."

5. Genitive plural masculine first aorist participle passive of *sunágō* from *sún,* "together," and *ágō,* "to bring."

The only reason Paul entered into the picture here is because it took the Corinthian believers so long to act in this case. Had they acted on their own, no doubt Paul would have commended them for it.

Paul was writing from Ephesus as an apostle who had labored among the Corinthians. He considered them to be his children in the faith. Yet he did not make an arbitrary decision. He made a personal judgment which he then made known to them, but he did not want to impose this on the local congregation to which evidently he attributed the responsibility of solving its own problems. They were to gather together at a special meeting and discuss this matter and ask the enablement of the Holy Spirit so that they could make the right decision. Paul recognized that it was not his prerogative to excommunicate someone from a local assembly. No one man, even though he was an apostle, apparently had such authority. A local congregation is autonomous and must take its own disciplinary action.

The Source of Paul's Authority

Now we must go to verse four in which Paul reveals the authority by which he has decided to recommend the action of delivering such a one to Satan: "In the name of our Lord Jesus Christ." The preposition *en*, "in," indicates "by means of the name of Jesus Christ" or "in union with the name of Jesus Christ," that is, with the concurrence of all that for which the name of Jesus stands. "The name" refers to the character of the Lord Jesus. The Lord would never tolerate such acts of fornication by any member of the local assembly. Paul implies that Christ is his Lord and He is their Lord as well, and therefore His actions should be their actions concerning this man.

Discipline Is the Prerogative and the Duty of the Local Congregation

Although Paul could have arrived at a decision and judgment of the young man's incestuous act on his own, this was not a matter that affected only him, but also affected the people of the local congregation.

Sometime ago a newspaper printed an article about a woman who bought a baby lion to be her pet. It was cuddly and loveable. The two became great friends. But as the animal grew larger, her friends began to fear for her safety and warned her to free it.

"Never," replied the woman. "He is as gentle and harmless as a kitten."

Alas, the day came when the real nature of the beast erupted. The woman was found torn to shreds.

Tolerance of our fellow human beings is a good thing, but tolerance of evil is certainly not taught in God's Word. He wants His body to be pure and holy, and sin must be cast out of the local congregation.

LESSONS:

1. Every sin, past or present, must be dealt with. Sweeping it "under the rug" is not the answer for the sinful individual or for the church.
2. The members of the church were to gather together, discuss the matter, and come to a decision regarding a sinful member. It was not a matter to be kept only by church leadership, but to be the entire congregation's concern.
3. The church needed to be fully dependent upon the power and enablement of the Lord Jesus Christ, not deciding serious matters on their own.
4. Paul writes the Corinthians from Ephesus as an apostle who has labored among them, considering them his children in the faith. And he gives them a personal judgment without imposing it on the local congregation.

5. In 1 Corinthians 5:4 Paul states that it is "in the name of our Lord Jesus Christ" that he has the authority to recommend the action of disciplining this incestuous one.
6. Tolerance should be given to people, not to their evil deeds; sin must be thrown out of the church.

1 Cor. 5:4, 5 — Who Can Remit or Retain Sins?

In the name of our Lord Jesus Christ, when ye are gathered together, and my spirit, with the power of our Lord Jesus Christ, to deliver such an one unto Satan for the destruction of the flesh, that the spirit may be saved in the day of the Lord Jesus.

The expression "with the power of our Lord Jesus Christ" really does not apply to the gathering together of the believers in Corinth or to Paul's spirit, but rather to the delivering of the incestuous young man to Satan. That cannot be done apart from the power of the Lord Jesus.

This Scripture is definitely related to the authority of believers to dismiss or forgive sins and to retain such, as we read in John 20:22, 23 where our Lord said, "Receive you the Holy Ghost: whose soever sins you remit, they are remitted unto them; and whose soever sins you retain, they are retained."

To whom exactly did the Lord give authority to remit and retain sins? On carefully examining this entire section in John's Gospel, we observe that it has to do with the appearance of the Lord Jesus Christ after His resurrection. The passage includes all the disciples who were present and not the eleven only. Verse nineteen states: "Then the same day at evening, being the first day of the week, when the doors were shut where the disciples were assembled for fear of the Jews, came Jesus and stood in the midst, and said unto them, Peace be unto you."

In the parallel passage in Luke's Gospel, it is explicit that the apostles were not alone. Let us look at Luke 24:33: "And they rose up the same hour, and returned to Jerusalem, and found the eleven gathered together, and them that were with them." It is certain, then, that when Jesus spoke the words of our text, other believers were also present, perhaps even all the believers in Jerusalem, since their number was very small. Undoubtedly Mary Magdalene, mentioned in John 20:18, and the other disciples must have been present with them.

John 20:23 provides conclusive evidence that Jesus Christ did not confer any formal gifts on the apostles, for the power to remit and retain sins was never exercised in a literal and authoritative sense by any of the apostles. It is apparent that they did not think that Christ conveyed such authority to them alone. Surely the apostles would have utilized such tremendous authority if they had it, and the fact that they did not exercise such authority seems to indicate that no such authority was ever given them. They understood that not only apostles but also all believers (Luke 24:33) had the Holy Spirit within them (John 16:7; 20:22) to discern genuine repentance activated by the Holy Spirit and to declare the removal of sin—not by them but by Christ Himself. This is especially so since just before He spoke these words of John 20:23 He breathed on them a fresh infilling of the Holy Spirit, thus enabling them to comprehend what otherwise could have been misunderstood and misapplied. Accordingly, even in this particular instance of incest in Corinth, the apostle Paul does not act solely, but shares that authority with the local believers of that congregation.

Delivering the Sinner to Satan

To whom should the congregation, along with the apostle Paul, deliver such a sinner? "To Satan for the destruction of the flesh."

Such an expression is also found in 1 Timothy 1:6, 7 where Paul writes concerning those who, "having swerved have turned aside unto vain jangling [or vain words], desiring to be teachers of the law; understanding neither what they say, nor whereof they affirm."

Continuing in verse twenty Paul says, "Of whom is Hymenaeus and Alexander; whom I have delivered unto Satan, that they may learn not to blaspheme." Here we find Paul did this himself because no local congregation was involved. It is apparent, therefore, that such delivering to Satan can be done by an individual gospel worker or believer.

The responsibility of expelling the incestuous young man from the local Corinthian congregation was solely that of the congregation. This is shown by Paul's statement in verse two: "And you are puffed up, and have not rather mourned, that he that has done this deed might be taken away from among you." That the local congregation must exercise discipline is further shown by the use of the second person plural, *exareíte*, put away, in verse thirteen: "You [pl.] put away from among yourselves that wicked person." Of course, this second reference to disciplinary action applies generally to any congregation in which there is a need for such. It has primary reference to this particular case. No apostle on his own and no bishop or superintendent of any church body has authority to excommunicate a member of a local group. This is the task of the local church itself.

Apostolic Authority

There is, however, something that a local church cannot do by itself and which belongs to the realm of apostolic authority.

This is mentioned in verse five: "To deliver such a one unto Satan for the destruction of the flesh." Paul did not say that the Corinthians could do this themselves. The main verb in verses three through five is *kékrika*, "I have judged," and the object of this verb is the infinitive *paradoúnai*, "to deliver." The judgment regarding the offender was a personal decision of Paul's which, however, had to be implemented by an action of the local congregation. They were to act as if his own spirit were present, and with the power of the Lord Jesus Christ. Ultimately, however, the action of the congregation was based upon apostolic authority.

That apostolic authority was an underlying factor in ecclesiastical discipline is demonstrated in the case of Hymenaeus and Alexander. When Paul speaks of their being delivered to Satan, he states that he himself did this (1 Tim. 1:20). Delivering these individuals to Satan was obviously something the apostle could do on his own with apostolic authority. He does not say in this case that he acted in the power of the Lord Jesus Christ. Such authority was inherent in him as an apostle, and he understood the exercise of that authority to be his apostolic prerogative.

We may conclude, therefore, that no local congregation should ever assume to exercise a prerogative that belongs only to an apostle, that of delivering anyone to Satan.

What Does "Deliver to Satan" Mean?

Before we determine whether that was done in the case of any others, however, we must determine what this expression "deliver to Satan" means. Such phraseology was foreign to the activity of a local Jewish synagogue, and the apostle Paul did not borrow it from Jewish practices.

Commentator F. Godet gives an apt illustration. He says that the apostle here resembles a mother crying to God for her prodigal son and saying to Him, "My God, strike him, strike him even to the death, if necessary, if only he will be saved!"

In reality the Corinthian young man was under the influence of Satan already. His sin of fornication was not inspired by God but by Satan. His continuing in the local Christian congregation, however, gave this young man and the Christian community in Corinth the idea that one could sin in this way and still be considered a member or affiliate of the Christian church in good standing. For a believer to fall into sin is bad enough, but to tolerate it as something acceptable by God and the congregation of local believers is far worse. This was the weakness of the Corinthian church, and unfortunately it is the situation of the church of the twentieth century. How many local congregations today have the moral courage and spiritual insight to put out of their midst a flagrant sinner?

LESSONS:

1. Not only apostles, but all believers had the Holy Spirit within them to discern genuine repentance and declare the removal of sin by Christ Himself.
2. Delivering a person to Satan can be done by an individual gospel worker or beliver.
3. Ultimately the congregation's act to deliver someone to Satan was based on apostolic authority.
4. A local congregation should never exercise a prerogative that belongs only to an apostle, that of delivering someone to Satan.
5. It is bade enough for a believer to fall into sin, but to tolerate it as acceptable by God and the local believers is far worse. This weakness of the Corinthian church is unfortunately the situation twentieth century church as well.

1 Cor. 5:5 | *The Buffeting of Satan*

To deliver such a one unto Satan for the destruction of the flesh, that the spirit may be saved in the day of the Lord Jesus.

Let us not place fornication in isolation as if it were worse than many other sins which we tolerate in our local congregations. In Romans 1:20–32 Paul includes in the same class some sins which we may be prone to overlook. Which honest child of God, reading the following list, would not find at least one or two categories where he would fit? "Being filled with all unrighteousness, fornication, wickedness, covetousness, maliciousness, full of envy, murder, debate, deceit, malignity, whisperers, backbiters, haters of God, despiteful, proud, boasters, inventors of evil things, disobedient to parents, without understanding, covenant breakers, without natural affection, implacable, unmerciful: who knowing the judgment of God, that they which commit such things are worthy of death, not only do the same, but have pleasure in them that do them." If all who commit any of the above mentioned sins were expelled from our churches today, there would hardly be anybody left!

The young man whom Paul was considering was already under the influence of Satan, but at the same time he himself and others were under the illusion that he was still in good standing in his church. Paul said it must be one or the other; therefore, deliver him to Satan whose bidding he was doing by committing acts of fornication with his stepmother. Do not allow him or others, by overlooking his sin, to think that he is a well-accepted member. The acceptance of a member to a congregation is a serious responsibility for the local church. One is appalled today at the ease with which professing Christians are accepted as members of congregations. Potential members ought to be examined carefully and their lives scrutinized before they are pronounced members in good standing. Unfortunately, however, many congregations are so eager to expand their church membership that they overlook sin.

Sidestepping Responsibility

I am familiar with an example that is worth recalling in this instance. A certain man was employed by a Christian organization. Since he was in financial distress, this organization lent him several thousand dollars in order to buy a house. He promised to pay it back in installments. Meanwhile, he left the employment of this Christian organization. Finally he declared bankruptcy, but the bankruptcy law permitted him to keep his house. Not many months later he sold the house at a profit far in excess of the amount he owed. When he was asked whether he was going to repay the Christian organization from which he had borrowed his down payment, his reply was, "I have been legally released from my obligations, and, therefore I don't owe it anymore." Not much later the wife of this man was observed at a shopping center with one of the most luxurious cars available. The Christian congregation to which this man belonged did absolutely nothing to discipline him for defrauding a Christian organization through the legal maneuver of declaring bankruptcy.

Was this a private matter or in reality one that affects the church to which such a person belongs? The local church, by avoiding discipline, gives the idea that such practices are acceptable to Christianity. But tolerating such actions is almost as bad as doing them (Rom. 1:32).

Would that congregations which claim to be preaching the gospel would have the moral stamina to do what the Corinthian congregation did, to expel such a one and to deliver him to Satan! By allowing such a member to remain in good standing, the church gives him and others the idea that his action is proper. Most likely the man will never repent of his sin unless the local congregation takes action and he is told that he is under the power of Satan. Let us not forget that in 1 Corinthians 6:10 thieves and covetous people are equated with the fornicators mentioned in verse nine. The same is also found in Ephesians 5:5: "For this you know, that no whoremonger [*pórnos*], nor unclean person, nor covetous man who is an idolater, has any inheritance in the kingdom of Christ and of God." In 1 Timothy 1:10 even liars are placed in the same category as whoremongers: "For whoremongers, for them that defile themselves with mankind, for menstealers, for liars, for perjured persons, and if there be any other thing that is contrary to sound doctrine."

Delivering to Satan Means Allowing One to Be Where He Fits

This delivering to Satan is something like the father of the prodigal son delivering his son to a place and a practice completely separate from the philosophy of life of the father's house. The son knew perfectly well that he would lack the freedom to practice a riotous lifestyle at home, and so he took off. The father delivered him to its evil influences, but always hoped and prayed that he would repent and return home.

This father may have been in a dilemma such as we see all too often today. Many a Christian family has had to forbid their son or daughter from bringing their lovers into their bedrooms or using drugs at home. It is quite common in such cases for the erring child to leave home, but can a godly parent give the appearance of condoning the sinful lifestyle because he or she is afraid the child will leave? No, he can only deliver the young person over to the evils of Satan and wait and pray as the father of the prodigal son did. Paul's attitude toward the young man who was committing fornication was similar. He had to be separated from the church, and during this period of separation and reaping the consequences of his choice, the apostle hoped he would repent of his sin.

Delivering someone to Satan by an apostle did not mean reckless abandonment to the hands of Satan, but rather permission for Satan to buffet the sinner by allowing him to reap the physical consequences of his sinful nature. Thus the sinner, realizing that sin does not pay, might come to his senses and turn from his self-destructive path of evil. There is probably no sin that does not leave its own grievous consequences even during the lifetime of the perpetrator.

Fortunately, Satan's power is limited by God, and He cannot do whatever he wants. He can only do what God permits him to do up to a certain point. This is perfectly illustrated by the example of Job. The Lord, after hearing Satan's proud words that he could do anything he wished with Job, said to him: "Behold, all that he has is in your power; only upon himself put not forth your hand. So Satan went forth from the presence of the Lord" (Job 1:12). Satan was given permission to go so far and no farther. What Satan did to Job was to afflict him physically. Job had a mortal body subject to sickness and suffering, but his spirit was that of a righteous man which Satan could not touch.

Physical suffering and illness was due to man's yielding to Satan's temptation. Although God gave man the power of choice, He could never be held responsible for his fall. Man's freedom to yield to sin is not eradicated at conversion. When the believer chooses to sin, he cannot claim exemption from the preset consequences of his choice. Delivering such a person to Satan means allowing that person to reap the consequences of his own sinful choice. If a person engages in immoral sexual activities, he may suffer the buffeting of Satan through venereal disease or AIDS, but regardless of how much Satan may make him suffer, God alone determines the extent of that suffering (Heb. 2:14).

Delivering someone to Satan can cause him to realize the consequences of his sin in order that he may repent and return to his Father's house. It is a redemptive deliverance to the one whom man has chosen to temporarily please. God may be saying, "Let Satan show you how dearly you pay for serving him." Being under the power of Satan can be very painful. How much easier it is, and more pleasant, to flee from sin rather than enjoy its pleasure for a season but reap its consequences for an eternity.

Satan Zeros in on Believers

Paul habitually perceived pain, disease, loss, and obstruction as the work of the evil spirit. In illicit sexual desire, it is actually Satan who tempts us by taking advantage of our weakness (1 Cor. 7:5).

Satan Is Never Satisfied

One thing is certain, Satan will take full advantage of the limited power granted to him by almighty God, especially in regard to the believer. Second Corinthians 2:11 is especially noteworthy: "Lest Satan should get an advantage of us: for we are not ignorant of his devices." In other words, Satan would always like to go one step farther in his destructive work upon the believer, but he is not permitted by God who controls even Satan.

Satan Makes Sin Sweet at the Beginning

Paul tells us in 2 Corinthians 11:14 that Satan is transformed into an angel of light. How does he do that? By giving us a temptingly sweet taste of the satisfaction of sin, but not allowing us to see its end results. That is exactly what happened in the Corinthian case of incest. Why shouldn't he and his stepmother express their love to each other? It was a "genuine" love between them and their sexual desires were only normal, so they reasoned. There are those in our day who say that fornication is sinful only if done with an unwilling partner. According to God's Word, fornication is any act of sexual indulgence outside of legitimate marriage. To have sex with anybody other than one's spouse is a hideous sin. The Bible is very specific about this, but Satan leads his victims deeper and deeper into sin with the tantalizing desire for satisfaction and happiness. Sin never satisfies. The more one sins, the more he desires it, but the less it satisfies by creating a bottomless desire for even more sin. The New Testament has a word to describe such an insatiable desire for sin. It is the word *asélgeia* which is often translated as "lasciviousness" (Mark 7:22; 2 Cor. 12:21; Gal. 5:19; Eph. 4:19; 1 Pet. 4:3; Jude 1:4) and "wantonness" (Rom 13:13; 2 Pet. 2:7).

Satan Can Inflict Sickness if Allowed by God

In Second Corinthians chapter twelve, Paul recounts his experience of being caught up to the third heaven. Paul might have been puffed up with pride after such a supernatural experience. In order that he might remain humble, the Lord gave Satan the authority to inflict a certain illness upon Paul which he chose to call "a thorn in the flesh." In addition, he calls it "the messenger of Satan to buffet me." The agent of the disease was Satan, but the purpose for which God permitted it was beneficial and redeeming, for it kept Paul humble. "Lest I should be exalted above measure," God permitted Satan to afflict me, says the apostle.

No one is beyond Satan's reach. Even our Lord Himself was tempted by him. Satan wanted Jesus to take a shortcut to obtaining the ultimate rule of the world. He tempted Jesus to avoid the cross but without the cross there would have been no resurrection. Can we conceive of Christianity without the resurrection? Impossible! It would have been a common religion, as are all other religions in the world today.

Satan especially seeks to entrap those who try to please God. A believer, however, delivered to Satan is not abandoned by God. He is permitted to suffer in the hands of Satan, as this incestuous young man did, so that having experienced the sufferings resulting from sin and the condemnation by his fellow believers, he would return to moral conduct.

Satan's Full Measure Creates a Desire for God

We usually attribute adversity to Satan. Often he interferes with what we plan to do for God. In 1 Thessalonians 2:18 Paul wrote: "Wherefore we would have come unto you, even I Paul, once and again; but Satan hindered us." Yet through Satan's hindrance, God's plan was fulfilled.

Luke 13:10–17 records the story of the woman who suffered with an issue of blood for eighteen years. Her suffering was not due to unbelief. She was, in fact, called "a daughter of Abraham." Yet, in spite of it she was suffering. Our Lord, however, said of her, "Whom Satan has bound, lo, these eighteen years." But He goes on to say that what Satan bound, He came to loose: "Be loosed from this bond" (Luke 13:16). Therefore, it is inconceivable for us to conclude that Christ, or Paul, would deliver anybody to Satan for his eternal destruction.

It is true that the one who tempts us is Satan as Paul expresses in 1 Corinthians 7:5: "That Satan tempt you not for your incontinency." But in 1 Corinthians 10:13 Paul declares a wonderful truth: "There has no temptation taken you but such as is common to man: but God is faithful, who will not suffer you to be tempted above that you are able; but will with the temptation also make a way to escape, that you may be able to bear it."

What Is the Destruction of the Flesh?

For what purpose did Paul decide to deliver this young man to Satan? The purpose is indicated by the expression "for the destruction of the flesh." What does this mean?

The first thing that we must determine is the meaning of the word *flesh* as it is used here. Some hold that it means the fleshly, natural life of this young man, his sinfulness, and that he was delivered to Satan so that he might give up his sin. But would Satan cause anyone to give up sin? Impossible. Satan encourages people to sin, especially believers whom he pursues relentlessly.

The Pharisees accused Christ of casting out devils by the power of the devil. Christ's answer was, "How can Satan cast out Satan?" Is it possible that Satan would use his power to liberate people from his own power (see Luke 11:15–20)? The Pharisees had become unreasonable in their fanaticism.

Religious fanaticism can be a tool in Satan's hand. Consider, for example, the case of a priest who asserted that only his denomination had the truth and was skeptical of all others. When an evangelist of another denomination held revival services nearby, the priest denounced the evangelist and warned the people against the revival as though it were the work of the devil. A peasant boy, however, turned to the priest and said, "Ah, Sir, it must be a new devil then, for that's not the way the old devil used to make the people behave."

Returning now to the main point, we conclude that with God's permission, Satan sometimes afflicts people with extreme pain, and happily—no thanks to Satan—they turn to

God in desperation. And God, we may be sure, inclines His ear to their cries. We may be equally certain, however, that if one continues in sin, Satan will buffet them all the more, inflicting suffering. This is especially true in the case of habitual fornicators. Fornication leads to inescapable consequences. At first it is full of pleasure, but in the end, it leads to disaster from which one may be rescued only by grace through repentance and renewed obedience.

At certain times, and then only as God allows, Satan afflicts people to an even greater and greater degree. In despair, they may turn to God. I am sure that more than one fornicator, having contracted a sexually transmitted disease such as AIDS, has called on the God on whom he once turned his back. We are suffering in our bodies because of Satan, and if we serve Satan, he will cause us to suffer that much more. Fornication has natural consequences that the fornicator cannot escape. In the beginning, the way seems so sweet, but the end is so bitter.

What Is Eternal Destruction?

The word *sárx*, "flesh," in this verse, does not stand for moral evil as some commentators have thought. It stands rather for physical life, referring to the human body as contrasted to the human spirit. Throughout the New Testament, with the exception of 1 Corinthians 15:39 and Revelation 19:18, *sárx*, or flesh, stands only for human flesh. The meaning of the word "flesh" in the verse under discussion is the same as in 1 Corinthians 7:28 where the apostle Paul describes the bodily affliction that marriage brings upon a husband or wife compared to the lack of such for a single person. We can, therefore, say that wherever *sárx* denotes the body, it stands in contrast to the inward man, the *pneúma*, "spirit," or the *kardía*, "heart." (see also Rom. 2:28, 29; Gal. 6:13; Eph. 2:11; Col. 2:13). It is the material part of man versus the spiritual. The first is temporary as it now exists, and the second is permanent. When the two separate at death, the spirit lives on. Together flesh and spirit denote the whole human personality, the one being material and the other immaterial (1 Cor. 7:34, 2 Cor. 5:3–5; 7:34). When used with the words "flesh" or "body," the spirit refers to that part of man which survives death (Matt. 27:50; Luke 8:55; 23:46; John 19:30; Acts 7:59; Heb. 12:23; 1 Pet. 3:18, 19; Rev. 11:11).

What Does the Destruction of the Flesh Mean?

The Greek word for "destruction" in this verse is *ólethros* (derived from the verb *olethreúō*, "to corrupt, to destroy," or from the obsolete verb *oléō* which means "to slay or wound") and pertains to the body here on earth. Paul said that the fornicator ought to be delivered to Satan so that his body might be identified with the consequences of physical suffering on this earth as a result of his fornication. Does one wonder, for instance, about AIDS and herpes and other forms of disease that may be sexually transmitted? In most cases, they are destruction brought upon the human body directly or indirectly as a result of the sin of fornication. It is Satan confirming the evil and torment of sin which leads to physical death. Of course, sin is never restricted just to the person committing it. It has rippling effects. It leaves its damaging influence upon innocent people as part of the corruption that has come upon the earth as the result of sin (Rom. 8:17–28). Paul aptly describes it as groaning for the day when both our environment and our bodies will be liberated not only from the guilt and power of sin but also from its very presence.

However, the diseases pertaining to fornication are not commonly contracted by those who abstain from sexual sin. Could this be merely a matter of chance or is God trying to tell us that in order to avoid the consequences of sexual sin encompassed in this one word "fornication" we should diligently avoid this pitfall?

Of course, we must exercise mercy toward those who suffer from the consequences of fornication, whether deserved or undeserved. That is what mercy (*éleos*) is—doing everything possible to alleviate the consequences of evil or sin. God, of course, does not cancel out the consequences of sin for then He would encourage greater license in sin. Always the eternal truth is, "the wages of sin is death" (Rom. 6:23). The opposite of death is *cháris*, "grace," which, unlike *éleos*, "mercy," deals with the character of man in transforming it. The gift of God which is eternal life is not the *éleos* or mercy of God, but the *chárisma*, or the result of grace. God wants us to be merciful toward those who suffer the inevitable consequences of fornication and never rejoice in their suffering. The devastating consequences of sin, however, in themselves have a corrective element. One can conclude then that Paul feels that this fornicator ought to be delivered to Satan so that he can do his destructive work upon his body here on earth in order that his soul might be saved. There are some people who cannot learn otherwise. They need physical suffering; they seem unwilling to learn in any other way that sin has grievous consequences. Are prisons maintained only to protect society from the criminal, or also to teach the criminal the error of his ways?

Ananias and Sapphira Suffered Destruction of the Flesh

We have a notable example of a couple who were punished in their bodies for committing a definitive sin. They were Ananias and Sapphira whose story is recorded in Acts 5:1–11. Their sin was pride and lying. They wanted to appear more generous than they were, and so they lied saying that they gave for the poor all the proceeds of the sale of a piece of land that belonged to them, while in fact they had given only part of it. The result of this lying was that both Ananias and Sapphira were subjected to physical death. Did Peter actually strike them dead? No, it was not Peter who did so, but Peter did deliver them to Satan. Ultimately, it was God's act since Peter had not been given the authority to terminate a life. Their physical lives were taken away from them so that their spiritual lives might be spared. They most likely were believers since they placed their belongings at the feet of the apostle, unless they were unbelievers who merely wanted to impress others with the idea that they were generous Christians (Matt. 7:21–23).

Believers May Physically Die if They Partake Unworthily of the Lord's Supper

There is another reference indicating that indeed God permits Satan to punish believers. It concerns those who came to the Lord's supper and partook of the elements unworthily. Of these, Paul said in 1 Corinthians 11:30: "For this cause many are weak and sickly [*árrōstoi*, sing. *árrōstos*] among you and many sleep [*koimṓntai* referring to the death of a believer]." Two words referring to sickness are used together in this verse—*astheneís* and *árrōstoi*—and the only way that they are differentiated in the translation is through the words "weak" and "sickly." The word *asthenḗs* (sing.), however, is for the most part translated as "sick" and sometimes as "weak" or "feeble." It is made up of the negative *a* and *sthénos*, "strength," meaning "without strength." It may refer to either physical weakness or weakness with regard to spiritual things (see also Matt. 26:41; Mark 14:35; Rom. 5:6; 1 Cor. 9:22). The adjective *árrōstos*, "sick," is used only four times: Matthew 14:14; Mark 6:5, 13; 16:18; 1 Corinthians 11:30. It is derived from the negative *a* and *rhṓstos*, which in turn comes from *rhṓnnumi*, which is from *rhōnnúō*, "to strengthen." That *árrōstos* refers to physical sickness is made clear from its use in Mark 6:13: "And they cast out many devils [demons], and anointed [*ḗleiphon* from *aleíphō*, to rub] with oil many that were sick [*arrṓstous*] and healed them." Here we have two kinds of healing. The casting out of demons which was the liberation from spiritual powers, and the rubbing of sick bodies with oil which indicates that they were physically ill.

In 1 Corinthians 11:30, where both words are used, we must attribute *astheneís* as referring to general weakness, and *árrōstoi* as referring to those suffering specifically from physical sicknesses. The substantive *arrōstía* refers to a lingering ailment, a degenerate state of health, and therefore the KJV translation as "sickly" is correct. This helps us to understand 1 Corinthians 5:5 as referring to bodily or physical sickness with the expression "destruction of the flesh." The fornication of this man, Paul indicates, will eventually produce bodily sickness. The mortality of our flesh originated with Satan himself who tempted Adam and Eve into obeying him rather than God. God has preset the consequences of man's disobedience as sickness which leads to ultimate death. Thus, since Satan persuaded Eve to sin, bodily corruption came upon mankind as a result of this surrender to evil. Ever since, man's body has been corruptible and mortal (Rom. 6:12; 8:11; 1 Cor. 15:53, 54; 2 Cor. 4:11; 5:4).[1] Therefore Satan, who originally brought about this condition upon mankind, is the one who can, with God's permission, inflict it to an even greater degree on individuals. We are suffering in our bodies because of Satan, and if we yield to Satan, he will cause us to suffer that much more. Fornication has its natural consequences that the fornicator cannot escape.

The Power of God Over the Power of Satan

Hebrews 2:14 sheds light into Satan's dominion in regard to death. Here is how the KJV translates this verse: "Forasmuch then

---

1.Such corruptibility of the human body is expressed with the word *phthartós* (Rom. 1:23; 1 Cor. 15:54).

as the children are partakers of flesh and blood, he also himself likewise took part of the same; that through death he might destroy him that had the power of death, that is, the devil."

Here the apostle speaks of Christ's incarnation. He became partaker of flesh and blood. "The Word [*Lógos*] became flesh" (John 1:1, 14). He brought redemption to mankind "through [His] death." The death of Jesus Christ was made necessary as a result of Satan's tempting Eve to sin. The fact that man is spiritually dead is due to Satan, for the predicted consequences of sin cannot be cancelled.

The translation of Hebrews 2:14 is misleading because it translates the latter part of the verse by giving to the Greek participle *échonta*, "having" (which is the pres. tense), the past tense: ". . . that through death [Christ's death] he [Jesus Christ] might destroy him [Satan] that had the power of death, that is the devil."

The correct translation of *échonta* (translated "had") is "having" or "who has." The devil still has this power. He has not been deprived of it. Hebrews was written about A.D. 69 while First Corinthians was written in A.D. 57. The counsel Paul gave the Corinthian church to deliver this immoral young man to Satan for the destruction of the flesh was true then and continues to be true until such time as our present bodies shall be changed and receive incorruptibility (1 Cor. 15:53, 54).

There is no one, believer or unbeliever, whose body during this life is exempt from corruptibility and death. This has been the case since the fall of man (Gen. 3:1–13). Truly Satan in a certain restricted and specified way not only had the power of sin and death, but still has it.

It is unfortunate that even modern translations of the New Testament such as the NASB and the NKJV translate the present participle *échonta*, "having," in Hebrews 2:14 with the past tense, thus giving the impression that the power of the devil over death has been taken away. What Satan had before, he still has. That had not happened between Paul's writing of 1 Corinthians 5:5 and the book of Hebrews. What Paul said Satan would do with the immoral young man still applies today within God's limitations.

Just What Power Does Satan Have?

We now come to the second Greek word which is inadequately translated as "power" in the phrase referring to the devil having "the power of death."

Although the NIV has corrected the *échonta*, "having," by rendering it "who holds" referring to the devil, yet it translated the Greek word *krátos* as "power" as does also the KJV, the NASB, and the NKJV. The word *krátos* means "dominion" and not "power." It refers to a prevalent state of affairs and not to power (*dúnamis*, "strength" to accomplish something at will) or authority (*exousía*, "ability," the right and the might to do something). The death of Christ was not a victory for Satan. He did not take the life of Jesus. Satan never had power and authority over the lives of people. God always had and still has that. Jesus Christ himself expressed this in His declaration in Revelation 1:18 as having "the keys of hell [*Hades*] and of death." He did not state that He had these keys, but that He still has them.

What does Satan have then? The dominion (*krátos*) over the prevailing state of affairs. We all die because of his tempting Eve and Adam to sin (Rom. 5:12). Specifically, Satan is given permission to bring about physical calamities upon sinners who are believers out of fellowship with the Lord. God gives him that specific permission at times to accomplish His will. When Satan was permitted to bring about affliction upon Job it was restricted (Job 1:12). Satan never planned that Job would be more intimately attached to God. But Job, said, "Though he slay me, yet will I trust in him" (Job 13:15).

God does not directly bring such suffering upon men. Suffering and death are in the domain of Satan. We suffer and die because of him, but his power is restricted.

We must never forget that Satan is called the "ruler of the darkness of this world" (Eph. 6:12), but God is the ruler over all. The first word pertaining to the unseen demonic principalities of the world is *kosmokrátōr*, "the one who has dominion of the world." It derives from the word *kósmos* which in this instance means the world of wickedness and darkness; and *krátōr*, meaning the one who has dominion. *Krátōr* is related to *krátos*, "dominion," which is the very word found in Hebrews 2:14 and translated "power."

Who Is Ruler over All?

When it comes to God and Jesus Christ, we find another word, *pantokrátōr*, used which is usually translated in the KJV as "almighty" (2 Cor. 6:18; Rev. 1:8, 4:8; 11:17; 15:3; 16:7, 14; 19:15; 21:22) and "omnipotent" (Rev. 19:6). That word derives from *pán*, "all," which refers to each thing individually and all of them put together, and *krátōr*, "one who has dominion." Thus we see that Satan has dominion over the world (*kósmos*), "the evil world where sin and darkness prevail," but God has dominion over all including Satan. God is the One who instructed Paul to tell the Corinthian church to deliver the incestuous young man to Satan.

God is the One who gave the authority to Peter to strike Ananias and Sapphira dead. This God inspired Paul in writing to the Corinthian church to instruct it that there is the possibility that those who participate in the Lord's Supper unworthily could become physically ill and die (1 Cor. 11:29, 30).

There is often, however, an eternal benevolence resulting from the buffeting of Satan when it comes to believers. This is alluded to in the second statement of 1 Corinthians 5:5: ". . . that the spirit may be saved in the day of the Lord Jesus."

In the case of Paul's thorn in the flesh which must have been some sort of physical ailment (2 Cor. 12:5–7; Gal. 4:12–15), Satan is said to have been involved. Nevertheless, as a result, Paul experienced the grace of God more intimately.

The Benevolence of Physical Punishment

At the end of this verse, Paul stated that the reason the incestuous young man should be delivered to Satan for the destruction of the flesh was not merely that he should experience punishment, but also for redemptive purposes: "that the spirit may be saved in the day of the Lord Jesus." This phrase is introduced by the Greek word *hína* which is better translated "so that" or "for the purpose of." It is evident that *pneúma*, "spirit," stands in contradistinction to the flesh or the body as we know it here on earth.

The first word that we must examine in this phrase is the verb *sōthḗ*, "may be saved."[2] The verb *sṓzō* means to save or to deliver from evil or danger. The adjective *sṓos* means "safe, sound."

Another meaning is to make whole or heal of some bodily sickness. In this sense it is applied to the miraculous cures wrought by Christ and His apostles (see Matt. 9:21, 22; Mark 6:56; Acts 4:9). As these miraculous cures were emblems and pledges (see Acts 4:10, 12) of spiritual deliverance from sin and death through Christ, so the verb "to save" means also to save from sins, that is to say from the guilt, dominion, and eternal punishment of sin (see Matt. 1:21; Luke 7:48, 50). This salvation actually commences here on earth as Christians enter

---

2. *Sōthḗ* is the third person singular first aorist subjunctive passive of *sṓzō*.

a state of salvation in this present life (see Luke 7:50; 1 Cor. 15:2; Eph. 2:8; 1 Pet. 3:21).

It must now be determined which of these definitions pertains to the verb *sōthē̃*, "may be saved," in 1 Corinthians 5:5. Undoubtedly it is the first meaning, which is to deliver from danger and which refers to a specific time in the future. Also, the passive voice of this verb indicates that it was not this man who was going to save himself, but he was going to be saved by someone other than himself which is, of course, God.

Although the translation includes the word "may" in the phrase "may be saved," there is no "maybe" about it. There is apostolic certainty that if this disciplinary action were taken by the local congregation of Corinth, and if Satan had an opportunity to wreak his destructive work upon the body of this fornicator, he would come to his senses and repent from his sin and return to the Lord even as the prodigal son had returned. Therefore, although the only way to express a subjunctive mood in English is through the expression "may be saved," the Greek indicates certainty, he will be saved. A better translation of the phrase is "for the purpose that the spirit be saved" or "that his spirit be saved."

The Priority of the Spirit over the Body

What will be saved? "The spirit." It was his spirit which had been saved and, as a result of that salvation, his body ought also to have been sanctified (1 Thess. 4:3, 7).

The spirit is one of the three constituent parts of man's personality (1 Thess. 5:23), the other two being the soul and the body. The spirit of man is the element whereby man communicates with God (John 4:23, 24; Rom. 1:9, 8:16; Gal. 6:18; 2 Tim. 4:22; Phile. 1:25). Only man possesses a spirit, and only man can be saved spiritually. Animals and other living things have a soul which gives them environmental consciousness, and a body which is the physical dwelling place of their souls. In man, however, there is not only a soul (*psuchē*), but also a spirit. Each human being has a spirit which gives him a God-consciousness, a soul which gives him self and environmental consciousness and a body in which both dwell.

The Lord Jesus Christ indwells our spirits (Rom. 8:9–11). He is said to also indwell our bodies since our bodies are the dwelling places of both our soul and our spirit. However, our present body is temporal while our spirit is eternal, for it survives the body's death (Rom 6:12; 8:11; 1 Cor. 15:53, 54; 2 Cor. 4:11; 5:4). When Jesus died, He commended His spirit to the Father (John 19:30). The human spirit begins its existence in the human body and soul, but lives independently of them after the dissolution of human existence as we know it here and now.

Our spirit can be saved while we are in this life if we repent of our sin and believe on the Lord Jesus Christ. This salvation is called "eternal life" (John 3:16), and only believers possess it.

Can Real Christians Sin?

In this state of salvation, however, no one is devoid of the possibility of sin (Rom. 7:20; 1 John 1:7; 2:2). That we can fall into sin is made clear by the apostle John in 1 John 2:1: ". . . if any man sin, we have an advocate with the Father, Jesus Christ the righteous." The verb here is *hamártē*, the aorist subjunctive of *hamartánō*, "to sin." It refers to falling into a sin. In verse one John expresses the desire that we may never sin: "My little children, these things I write unto you, that you sin not." The verb for "sin" is *hamártēte*, in the subjunctive aorist active, meaning that you may commit any sin at any time. The more we dwell in God's Word, the less chance there is of our committing sin. But on the other hand, John also states that "if we say that we have no sin [and here he means of any kind, now that we are saved], we deceive ourselves, and the truth is not in us" (John 1:8). And in verse ten John states: "If we say that we have not sinned [*hēmartḗkamen*, perf. indic. of *harmartánō*, to sin, indicating at any time and we are now reaping the consequences], we make him [God] a liar, and his word is not in us." There is no doubt that reference is made to us as believers.

But if we are true believers, we cannot fall into sin without being convicted about it, and conviction brings confession. Hence the assurance of forgiveness exists for a repentant and confessing believer who may fall into any sin, even as grievous as incest. "If we confess our sins, he is faithful and just to forgive us our sins and to cleanse us from all unrighteousness" (1 John 1:9), and this cannot exclude the sin of fornication.

The Holy Spirit Must Save the Sinner

What is needed in order to bring a believer who has sinned to conviction and confession? Of course, it is the activity of the Holy Spirit.

But in 1 Corinthians chapter five, the apostle Paul also champions the idea of public exposure of the sin of this young man for which there is ample and incontrovertible evidence. If this were not proven, Paul would have never written, "For I verily, as absent in body, but present in spirit, have judged already, as though I were present, concerning him that has so done this deed" (1 Cor. 5:3), which was followed by his instructions to the Corinthian church to discipline him by delivering him to Satan for the physical destruction of his body. As we stated earlier, the reason for this disciplinary action was for the specific purpose that his spirit be saved which implies that this young man was a saved believer. His spirit is mentioned in contrast to his body, and the verb here has the meaning, if negatively stated, "that his spirit may not perish." Paul did not want sin in the body to cause the spirit to lose its attachment to Jesus Christ.

The verb form is in the passive voice "that the spirit be saved," showing that he could not do it himself. Only the Holy Spirit could do it.

The same could not be said about this young man's stepmother because it seems likely that she was not saved since no particular concern is shown by Paul about her relation to the church. Evidently she was not a member of the local congregation. The young man, from all indications however, was a member, hence the recommended disciplinary action. The church should show concern about its own members, while for those without, the concern is to win them to Christ and not to discipline them since it has no jurisdiction over them.

The expression "the day of the Lord Jesus," also occurring in 2 Corinthians 1:14, is the same as the expression "the day of Christ" (see Phil. 1:6, 10; 2:16; 2 Thess. 2:2). This is the day when Jesus Christ will come to take away or snatch His own from the earth (1 Thess. 4:13–18) as compared to "the day of the Lord" or the day of God's judgment upon the earth (see Acts 2:20, 1 Thess. 5:2; 2 Pet. 3:10). Paul wanted to be certain the young man's spirit would be saved or participate in the blessing of those who will be raptured alive or resurrected at the coming of the Lord Jesus for His own. The verb "to be saved" has an eschatological meaning also in Matthew 10:22, 24:13: "but he that endureth to the end shall be saved."

LESSONS:

1. Although the young man who committed incest and others were deluded, thinking that he was still in good standing in the church, Paul asked that he be delivered unto Satan.
2. Allowing a sinning member to remain in good standing gives him and others the idea that the church considers his action proper. The man will likely never repent of his sin unless the church takes action and tells him that he is under Satan's power.

3. When an apostle delivered someone to Satan, it was not meant to abandon him to Satan, but rather to permit Satan to buffet him, allowing him to reap the consequences of his sin. Then hopefully the sinner would realize that sin does not pay and turn from his evil ways.
4. It is much easier and more pleasant to flee from sin than to enjoy its pleasure for a season but reap its eternal consequences.
5. Sin is never restricted to the person committing it. It has rippling effects. It leaves its damaging influence upon innocent people as part of the corruption that has come upon the earth as the result of sin.
6. The assurance of forgiveness exists for a repentant and confessing believer who may fall into any sin.

1 Cor. 5:6 | *Tolerance Is a Virtue—to a Certain Point*

Your glorying is not good. Know ye not that a little leaven leaveneth the whole lump?

The word translated "glorying" is the Greek word *kaúchēma* which is the result or subject matter of boasting. What you are boasting about is not good, Paul admonishes the Corinthians. To boast (*kaucháomai*) does not always have a bad meaning. If we boast in what Christ has done, it is good and proper ". . . He that glorieth [boasts], let him glory [boast] in the Lord" (1 Cor. 1:31).

In most of the instances the verb *kaucháomai* is translated "to glory," but in reality it is to boast or to speak out loudly and clearly about something. Some attribute the etymology of the word to *auchḗn*, "neck." It is to hold or stretch one's neck straight up at which position one can shout to be heard or seen by others. We have the English expression "to hold one's head high." It is the opposite of cowering in shame and silence.

There are two nouns derived from the verb *kaucháomai*. One is *kaúchēsis* which is the act of boasting and the other is *kaúchēma* which is the reason or subject matter of boasting. It is this latter word which is used in 1 Corinthians 5:6. Paul is saying "what you are boasting about is not good."

Now what were the Corinthians boasting about in this instance of a young, incestuous man? It was their tolerant attitude toward him as part of their congregation in spite of the fact that his sinful relationship was common knowledge both within and without the church. This is implicit in all that is said about the case. In verse one we have the expression "it is reported commonly," that is, it is heard everywhere. Today we would say it is all over the newspapers, radio, and television.

The church and its leadership evidently did nothing about it. Perhaps they decided to show tolerance since they did not want to push this case to its extreme. They could have excommunicated this incestuous young man and had nothing whatsoever to do with him. That would have been one extreme. The other extreme would have been to take the attitude that, after all, what one does at home is not the church's concern. The sanctuary has no business interfering in what takes place privately in the bedrooms of its members. The church in Corinth must have decided on the "it's none of our business" viewpoint. Paul takes the middle view. He wrote to the church in Corinth that they should concern themselves about this generally-known scandal concerning the private life and behavior of one of their church people. Today, we hear of so much immorality not only among church members, but preachers themselves. In recent times a very well known televangelist was convicted of certain misbehavior and is now in jail. But he is in jail for committing fraud in mishandling contributions and using them for his own personal benefit, not for having committed proven adultery. It just shows what our human justice considers a condemnable crime. Illicit sex is accepted.

How Far Should Christian Tolerance Go?

Such tolerance must not be found within the Christian church. Tolerance and forbearance are good virtues, but God has set moral standards that must be adhered to, and deviation from these standards are unacceptable in Christ's body.

To show tolerance toward a proven and unrepentant immoral person and his sin is not a virtue. It cannot result in the good of the church and its testimony. Yet whatever disciplinary action is taken by the church must exhibit a longsuffering and redemptive attitude toward the sinner involved. While we must do everything we can to preserve the purity of the local church, our disciplinary activity to correct a situation must also aim at the redemption of the individual or individuals concerned. For instance, one extreme action would have been, "Throw the bum out. He was never saved; there is no hope for him." The other attitude would have been, "Let the man alone. Why should we interfere? He is not our preacher. He is only a fellow member. Didn't Jesus say we should not judge lest we be judged [Matt. 7:1]? But for the grace of God, there go I!" That apparently became the prevailing attitude of the Corinthian Christians, and they considered it worth boasting about.

In Colossians 1:11 believers are urged to exercise patience (*hupomonē*), the ability to stand up under circumstances that are inevitable or providential. We accept and survive what we cannot prevent and what God allows as our circumstances of life. We find in Corinth a situation for which the church could not be held responsible. It was a situation that could arise in any church. In your church and mine we may not have known fornicators, but who knows how many hidden ones there are among us?

When the Lord Jesus wrote to the church in Ephesus in Revelation 2:2, He commended it for its works (*érga*), its hard toil (*kópos*), and patience (*hupomonē*). The church must exercise patience as it is attacked by worldly forces without and by known and unknown sinful practices within. Such sinful influences will affect it, but "the gates of hell [Hades] shall not prevail against it" (Matt. 16:18).

Longsuffering

The other virtue mentioned in Colossians 1:11 is *makrothumía* correctly translated in the KJV as "longsuffering." This is an attitude of concern toward people. Throwing the young sinner out of the church and shunning him was not an adequate answer to the problem. The church needed to show concern as to what would happen to him in the day of the Lord Jesus. Would he be among those who would take part in the rapture of the church as described in 1 Thessalonians 4:13–18, or would he be left behind to experience the wrath of God? This is the concern that Christians should show toward a sinner. While the sin and the social ecclesiastical situation that sin has created should be of immediate concern, the ultimate destiny of the sinner should also engage our attention and our action.

The Corinthian church acted as if in limbo, showing broad-mindedness which they thought was commendable, one more thing they could boast about.

There are other Greek words that indicate such a lenient attitude. One is *anochḗ*, "holding back, delay." That is the kind of attitude we frequently resort to when we face a difficult situation. Let us give time an opportunity to take care of it. That is the attitude of God toward unrepentant sinners as spoken of them: "Or despisest thou the riches of his goodness and forbearance [*anochḗ*] and longsuffering [*makrothumía*]; not knowing that the goodness of God leadeth thee to repentance" (Rom. 2:4). God could strike down all sinners, but He delays this action until they have had full opportunity to repent, and thus they can never say that they did not have a chance to turn from their sinful ways.

Consider what longsuffering and forbearance Jesus Christ showed toward Judas. He could have cast him out of the circle of the disciples, but He exercised longsuffering. Certainly Judas could never blame Jesus that He had not given him a chance.

In the case of the Corinthian church, however, there was danger that if one rotten apple were permitted to stay close to the good apples, the good apples would never restore the bad apple to health; rather, the bad apple would affect and spoil the rest. What is to be done at the discovery of the rotten apple? We do not ignore its presence. We take it out of the basket and isolate it to protect the others. This is the solution suggested by Paul in this case. Do not *give in* to the sinner, but do not *give up* on him. Deliver him to Satan to have his body destroyed, but have his spirit preserved, saved in the day of the Lord Jesus. Put him out, but do not show hatred. Show him that you love him and you are praying for his repentance and his return to the fellowship of believers. Paul is trying to protect the honor and testimony of the local church without abandoning the sinner.

Paul's Philosophy of Correction

In 2 Corinthians 10:1 Paul states his philosophy of action among the Corinthians by saying: "Now I Paul myself beseech you by the meekness and gentleness of Christ. . . ." Christ's meekness and gentleness is set as an example. What is meekness? It is *praótēs*, the virtue that stands between two extremes, the one of taking drastic measures without any concern as to the outcome and the other of showing complete indifference about a situation. *Praótes* ought to be our attitude in a situation such as the Corinthian church was facing.

The word *epieíkeia*, translated "gentleness," means "propriety" or that which is fit, reasonable, and proper in the case under discussion, the clemency needed to make the severity of the punishment redemptive. That was exactly the recommended action of Paul to be taken by the Corinthian church. Separate the rotten apple lest it contaminate the others, but do everything possible to be redemptive.

In fact, later, perhaps a few short months after writing 1 Corinthians, Paul is thought to be referring to the same young man who must have repented and was restored. In studying the context, one would come to the conclusion that the young man had a hard time being accepted again (2 Cor. 2:5–11).

What brought about his redemption? Putting him out of the local church, delivering him to Satan to suffer physically, produced the joyful result of repentance and restoration.

The same thing can happen today. Sin can bring about such devastating effects from venereal diseases and AIDS that it shocks people into repentance. Something of this kind may have happened to the anonymous, incestuous young man. His body was struck, but he was spared of death till he repented and was restored.

Evil Spreads

Leaven is a substance which produces fermentation, especially in the making of bread. It can be even a piece of already fermented dough which is mixed with other dough in order to repeat the process.

The English word is derived from the Latin *levare* meaning "to raise," while the Greek word for leaven, *zúmē*, is derived from *zéō* meaning "to warm, heat," or *zumóō*, meaning "to make to ferment." In a warm climate this fermentation is completed within twenty-four hours.

The commandment against the use of raised bread during the Passover week (Ex. 12:17; 13:7) was commemorative of Israel's beginning as a nation and of the putting away of all that was old.

Fermentation represented the process of corruption in the mass of the bread. This idea is found in the writings of the Greek essayist and biographer Plutarch, who says: "Now leaven is itself the offspring of corruption, and corrupts the mass [*phúrama*, used in 1 Cor. 5:7]." Bread with the taint of putrefaction was regarded as unfit for use in religious ceremonies.

As early pioneers traveled west across the United States in their covered wagons, they made their bread from sourdough since yeast was unavailable. Sourdough was, in fact, merely a mixture of flour and milk or water that had become polluted. By allowing the mixture to sit for several days, it would become contaminated with the live yeast bacteria in the air and ferment. In order to hasten the fermentation process, some old dough was added to the new mixture each time. As the mixture aged, it became more sour, and so did the bread—an apt illustration of the consequences of sin.

The Jews today on the evening of the first day of the Passover (the fourteenth day of Nisan) in accordance with the memorial custom, still carefully remove every trace of leaven which can be found in their house. Fresh dough kneaded with pure water is used in the preparation of the cakes of unleavened bread which are to be eaten during the holy week.

Leaven in the New Testament is applied to any element, influence, or agency which effects a subtle and secret change either for the better or for the worse.

The kingdom of heaven is likened to leaven, in a good sense, which is destined to penetrate and assimilate to itself those who receive it (Matt. 13:33; Luke 13:20f).

Here in 1 Corinthians 5:6 (see also Matt. 16:6, 11, 12; Mark 8:15; Luke 12:1; 1 Cor. 5:7, 8), it is used in a bad sense representing a sin considered insignificant but which, if tolerated and unchecked in a church or community, has a growing power of corruption.

Paul twice uses what has become a common saying, "A little leaven leavens the whole lump" (1 Cor. 5:6; Gal. 5:9). Since this is spoken in conjunction with the sins of the incestuous young man, the leaven must be interpreted as synonymous with this sin. Paul equates this sin with a "little leaven" to indicate not that he believes incest is a slight sin, but that only one member of the congregation was involved. Since this was the case, apparently the Corinthian church felt there was no danger. This is the reason the church did not take immediate steps of discipline and declaration of the seriousness of the situation. His own view about this sin is made clear by the verb he uses in verse three: "I have . . . judged."

To the Corinthian Church, the Sin of Incest Was Minor

The attitude of the Corinthian church is clarified by two statements Paul made. In verse two he wrote, "And you are puffed up, and have not rather mourned, that he that has done this deed might be taken from among you." The verb "you are puffed up" is *pephesiōménoi esté*.[1] The passive form of this verb here has a middle meaning, that is, you puff yourselves up, you inflate yourselves with pride. Dealing with an explosive issue such as this would shatter their pride. They wanted their reputation of broad-mindedness and leniency to remain undisturbed.

The second word that reveals their attitude toward this situation is the word *kaúchēma* which is the subject matter of boasting. The Corinthian church was proud that the still waters of peace and tranquility in their church were not disturbed.

And now the illustration Paul presents by referring to the sin as a "little leaven" reveals that they considered this matter a small sin, an undisturbing situation. "Little" is what you consider

---

1. *Pephesiōménoi* is the perfect passive participle of the verb *phusióō*, "to puff up."

this sin to be, Paul implies, but think of what a little leaven does. It takes just a little leaven to ferment the whole lump, or a kneaded mass.

In both instances of 1 Corinthians 5:6 and Galatians 5:9 Paul does not say the "large" lump or mass, but *hólon*, "all," the whole lump. It makes no difference how large the lump is, a little leaven is enough to ferment it. Even one small sin in the life of an individual affects the whole church. Nobody can escape unaffected and untarnished. But ignoring it is not the answer. While it may be a cancer that starts small, inevitably it grows and consumes the whole life of the church. It is better to go through the surgical trauma of excising the sin while it is small rather than having the whole body become infected.

LESSONS:

1. We must do everything to preserve the purity of the church; moreover, our discipline must aim at redeeming sinners.
2. After immediate attention is given to a sin and the social ecclesiastical situation that sin creates for a church body, our attention and action should be given to the ultimate destiny of the sinner.
3. Meekness (*praótēs*) stands between two extremes, that of taking drastic measures with no concern as to the outcome and that of showing complete indifference about a situation.
4. Perhaps a few short months after writing 1 Corinthians, Paul refers to a man who has repented and has been restored who is thought to be the same young man that committed incest with his stepmother in 1 Corinthians 5.
5. Paul calls the incest a "little leaven" because only one church member was involved, not because he believes incest is a slight sin.
6. No matter how large the lump, a little leaven is enough to ferment all of it. One sin in committed by an individual affects the whole church.

1 Cor. 5:7 | *Purging Out Evil*

Purge out therefore the old leaven, that ye may be a new lump, as ye are unleavened. For even Christ our passover is sacrificed for us:

The leaven was a symbol of the sin of incest of the young man who apparently was part and parcel of the Corinthian church. If he had not been related to the church, this was an empty command. To purge him out, he must have been part of the church.

The verb used for "purge" is *ekkathárate.*[1] It derives from *ek*, "out of," and *kathaírō*, "to cleanse from filth." *Kathaírō* is used with the meaning of pruning useless branches so that the useful branches may be made more productive (John 15:2). It also means to purify as in Hebrews 10:2. When the preposition *ek*, "out of," is used as a prefix, it means to remove an evil since evil affects others. It means to excise.

Evil is like cancer. On its discovery, there is only one thing to do, purge it out. But as the physician does this, he is careful not to affect the healthy part of the body on which the growth lies. The excising is remedial.

1.The aorist imperative active of *ekkathaírō.*

The verb *ekkatháirō* is used only one other time in Scripture: in 2 Timothy 2:21 where Paul says, "If a man therefore purge himself from these he shall be a vessel unto honor, sanctified, and meet for the Master's use, and prepared unto every good work." Now, what are "these" from which a believer ought to purge himself? The previous verse says, "But in a great house there are not only vessels of gold and of silver, but also of wood and of earth; and some to honor, and some to dishonor" (2 Tim. 2:20).

Timothy's illustration is a picture of the local Christian church. Ideally, all who are in it should be children of God who have received Christ (John 1:12). Believers in a church are of various degrees of maturity according to their conformity to the character and purposes of Christ. The mature sons who are led by His Spirit (Rom. 8:14) are called "vessels of gold and silver," precious metals. The immature children or babies (Gal. 4:1, 3; Eph. 4:14) are presented as vessels of wood or clay which are inexpensive materials and are also easily broken. That immature Christians are those in a local church congregation who are easily tempted and sometimes succumb to the desires of the flesh is implied in Paul's command to young Timothy in verse twenty-two: "Flee also youthful lusts." In a local church there are those who value and maintain moral sanctity and those who "play around" with lusts!

Separate Yourselves from the Immoral Ones

Now what is Paul's suggestion to Timothy in this pastoral epistle? When you see such lustful Christians and the church follows the course of apathetic silence in disciplining them, it would be better to remove yourself from them in order that you may maintain your own moral purity. Upon the detection of fire, try to put it out, but when you see you cannot do it, get out so that you yourself may not be burned.

What an indictment upon our local churches! How many times are admonitions heard on the moral behavior of the Christian in the midst of a world that deifies and encourages every form of immorality?

Paul advises the church in Corinth to purge itself of the one person in its midst who was well-known for his immorality. Are churches today willing to do this in order to maintain the purity of the church? And how many of our churches can do this purging in such a way that at the end the offender is also brought back in love and repentance (2 Cor. 2:5–11)?

Interestingly, Paul does not say "purge out the offender" but "purge out the old leaven." Leaven stands for sin or evil. It refers to the young man who had the incestuous relationship with his stepmother. The Corinthian church not only did not act redemptively by censuring its young man, but prided itself and boasted over its exercise of liberal tolerance (1 Cor. 5:2, 6). In essence, Paul says to the church, "You cannot shut your eyes to what is going on and pride yourselves over your liberal tolerance and forbearance. These are indeed graces to be practiced in proper contexts, but not in this one." How important it is to make proper judgments in the realistic situations of life! Here was a case where immediate, careful, and redemptive action was needed and not the practice of delay, toleration and compromise.

Keep Stomping Down that Old Serpent

Why does Paul designate the leaven as "old"? The Greek word is *palaián*, "the previous one." The word *palaiós* stands in contrast to *archaíos*, "original." God did not create man with a sinful nature, but in His image. However, He gave him the privilege of choice and clearly stated the consequences of disobedience. Man believed Satan instead of his Creator God and consequently fell. He allowed sin to enter into him and take control. When man believes on the Lord Jesus, he becomes a partaker of

God's nature (2 Pet. 1:4), a new creature. In 2 Corinthians 5:17 this new creation is called *kainēktisis*,[2] a qualitatively new creation. What happens to the previous nature? It is still in existence, but it is subjected to the Holy Spirit who indwells man. Paul expresses what it takes to keep his own old nature under control when in 1 Corinthians 9:27 he says about himself: "But I keep under my body and bring it into subjection." What is translated with the phrase "I keep under my body" is the verb *hupōpiázō* meaning "to hit under the eye" or give a black eye. This implies that when the sinful body of the believer tries to raise its ugly head and cause him to sin, he should hit it, or slap it down. Paul says this about himself, and we ought to do the same. Have you ever tried to kill a snake with your heel? You may stomp on its head, but it will raise it right back up. Again you must stomp on it, and again and again and again. It does not die easily. No wonder God called Satan "that old serpent" (Rev. 20:2).

And the Greek word translated "bring it into subjection" is the Greek verb *doulagōgṓ*, the contracted form of *doulagōgéō*, "to enslave," which is derived from *doúlos*, "slave," and *ágō*, "lead, bring," and which means to lead my body as if it were a slave. Paul counted his body as dead, for although it had physical existence, it had no will of its own (Rom. 8:10). Before we were received by God's Spirit, we had our behavior in the lusts of our flesh, fulfilling the desires of the flesh and of the mind (Eph. 2:3). That was our "old" nature. It is our duty to be on the alert to give it a black eye, to stomp on it to keep it down, and to control it as a slave and not allow it to lead us around. While we cannot deny that we have a sinful nature which is able to wreak devastation upon us, we must allow the Holy Spirit within us to deal it the blows necessary to keep it as a slave instead of allowing

---

2. *Kainḗ*, qualitatively new; *ktísis*, creation.

it to master us even for a passing time. It is a constant struggle and spiritual warfare.

While we have no power to purge others and make them clean, we can, by the grace of God, do this to ourselves. Paul does not tell those in the Corinthian church to "purge out" the young man. They may have excommunicated him, but that is never enough. The purging, the cleansing of sin must be our concern, but only the blood of Jesus can cleanse the individual, we cannot (1 John 1:9). In 2 Timothy 2:21 Paul said to Timothy, "If a man purge himself. . . ." The purging is something we each must do to our own selves and not to one another.

All that Paul recommended to the church was to deliver the sinful man to Satan to buffet him, to allow him to reap the full consequences of his sin as far as his body was concerned. He was to be brought to the realization that the Christian Church is not a haven of sinning believers who serve their bodies, but a fellowship of saints who hold their bodies in subjection.

Not Only New, But Better

The purpose of purging out the old leaven was that the local church might be a new lump. The word translated "new" here is *néon*, referring to something that did not exist before. *Néos* stands in contrast to *kainós* which is new but qualitatively different. When we are saved, we become a *kainḗ* creation or qualitatively different. We acquire God's nature which enables us to hold down and under control our old nature. But this preeminence of the spiritual over the carnal needs constant guarding and improving. This improvement is expressed by the verb *ananeóō* used only in Ephesians 4:23: "and be renewed in the spirit of your mind."[3] This is the positive result of our obedience

---

3 *Ananeoústhe,* the present infinitive passive used with a middle meaning implying it is something that we must do ourselves.

to the command in verse twenty-two: "That ye put off concerning the former conversation [conduct] the old man, which is corrupt according to the deceitful lusts." Our spirit is renewed as we take definitive steps to put off from our lives, from our former conduct, the old (*palaión*, "former" as in 1 Cor. 5:6 with reference to the old leaven) man. The spiritual renewal we experience is in direct proportion to the "putting off" which indicates that at any time we are tempted by deceitful lusts, we must put them away, one at a time.[4] Remember that "old serpent." We must keep stomping it down.

Cleansing Brings Improvement

"That you may be a new lump" therefore means that the church as a whole, the local church, may be a better church. Promptly and properly dealing with sin in the church will make the whole body of the church better. If it is neglected, however, sin will eventually spread and wreak havoc.

The word for "lump" is *phúrama* which is a kneaded mass, a mass of dough. Paul admonishes the Corinthian church not to allow bad leaven, sin, to mix in with the church because it will contaminate the whole church.

In Romans 9:21 we read, "Has not the potter power over the clay, of the same lump [*phúrama*] to make one vessel unto honor, and another unto dishonor?" Remember the illustration of Paul in 2 Timothy 2:20 about vessels that are gold and silver and wooden and earthen in the same house. Our bodies become honorable according to the influence and direction that we allow the immanent and transcendent Holy Spirit to give them.

4.*Apothésas,* the aorist infinitive middle of the verb *apotíthēmi,* "to put it away from oneself" (Eph. 4:22).

How we deal with a situation such as this one concerning a man in the church who fell into fleshly sin can make or break a church. What is the proper way to deal with it? Clean it out, purge out the old leaven, the sin of the former nature, after you have mourned over the situation and disciplined the sinner. Deliver him to Satan by asserting that his sin is of Satan and affirming that the wages of sin is death (Rom. 6:23). When the church confirms the Scriptures, then the redemptive operation of the Holy Spirit may result in the sinner's spirit being saved in the day of the Lord Jesus.

Christ's Sacrifice Is a Guarantee of the Church's Survival

The Corinthian church, in spite of its being carnal, was a church of redeemed, saved people. In 1 Corinthians 3:1 Paul said, "And I, brethren, could not speak unto you as unto spiritual, but as unto carnal, even as unto babes in Christ." In 1 Corinthians 13:11, Paul acknowledges that at one time he was a spiritual baby himself: "When I was a child [the word here is *nḗpios*, "babe" as in 1 Cor. 3:1], I spake as a child, I understood as a child [*nḗpios*], I thought as a child [*nḗpios*] but when I became a man, I put away childish [*nepíou*] things."

Here in 1 Corinthians 5:8, however, despite his reprimand of the Corinthian church, Paul does not refer to them as babies as he did in 1 Corinthians 3:1. Instead he calls them "unleavened" (*ázumoi* from the priv. *a*, meaning without, and *zúmē*, "leaven" in the sense of sin or corruptness, perverseness of life, doctrine, and heart [Matt. 16:6, 11; Mark 8:15; Luke 12:1]). All saved, born-again believers are to be "unleavened," no matter whether they are babies or spiritually mature. Paul might have said to the Corinthian church: "A sinful lifestyle does not characterize you. You are unleavened since, as a result of your faith, you died unto sin and you began to live unto God." "God forbid. How shall we that are dead to sin live any longer therein?"

(Rom. 6:2).[5] Every believer has died unto sin. The sin nature was killed by Christ's death. Romans 6:6 states it clearly and attributes it to Christ: "Knowing this, that our old [*palaiós*] man is crucified with him, that the body of sin might be destroyed, that henceforth we should not serve sin." What is translated "is crucified" is *sunestaurṓthē*, the aorist passive of *sustauróō*, "to crucify with." When we believe on the Lord Jesus Christ, not only do we have our sins cleansed with His blood (Rom. 3:25; 5:9), but Christ has crucified our old (*palaiá*) sinful nature with His own body and it no longer has preeminence. Nevertheless, Paul states in 1 Corinthians 15:31, "I die daily," and in 2 Corinthians 6:9, "as dying, and behold, we live." Christ did not eliminate the existence of the old nature, but He put it down and our spirit must constantly fight against it. We must kill the serpent of sin, our old nature.

Yet in spite of this struggle, we are unleavened; the nature of sin does not prevail in us. Paul recognized this about the Corinthian church in spite of the reprimand he gave them for tolerating sin in their midst.

Our Standing Is Due to Christ's Sacrifice for Us

In 1 Corinthians 5:7, there is a little adverb which is translated "as" in the KJV. The Greek is *kathṓs*, derived from *katá*, "according," and *hōs*, "as." *Kathṓs* should be translated "inasmuch as." Paul confirms the basic fact that the church as such was constituted of believers who were unleavened, meaning without the prevalence of the sin nature in them, although some were spiritual babies and carnal.

Paul then proceeds to state why they indeed had the "unleavened" nature. The conjunction *kaí*, translated "and," here has

---

5 *Apethánomen*, the aorist of *apothnḗskō*, "to die."

the meaning "indeed": "Indeed Christ is sacrificed for us." Through this statement, Paul deprives the Corinthians of the ability to take any credit to themselves. His politeness, however, is shown by the fact that he does not say, "For even Christ your passover is sacrificed for you." He includes himself and says "us." The fact that the Corinthians may have been in good standing was not due to their own goodness, but to the sacrifice of Christ for them, and also for Paul, for he himself says in Romans 3:20, "by the deeds of the law there shall no flesh be justified." However, in Romans 13:12 he does say that there is something we must do consequent to our justification which is to ". . . cast off the works of darkness, and let us put on the armor of light."

Inherent in the realization of the fall of one brother is the emergence of pride in our own standing. Look at him! He has fallen to the depth of degradation! We have never done anything like that!

Remember, Paul implies that our standing is due to Christ's sacrifice for us: "For indeed Christ our passover is sacrificed for us."

The phrase "is sacrificed" would be more accurately translated "was sacrificed."[6] In the New Testament it means to kill and offer in sacrifice. Reference is made here to Christ's sacrifice as God's Lamb. The two words "passover," which means a sparing, an immunity, and "Christ" are used in apposition to each other. What the Passover was for the Jews while they were in Egypt, Christ is for us. When the lamb was killed by the Jewish families and its blood sprinkled on the two side posts and on the upper door post of each Jewish house, the death angel of destruction passed

---

6. The verb *etúthē*, the aorist indicative passive of *thúō*, "to sacrifice."

over. As in the Passover, there was safety for the Jews in a strange land, so because of the shedding of the blood of Christ there is safety for the believers who are in the world. Christ is the Lamb without blemish and spot, sacrificed for us (1 Pet. 1:19). He is the door marked with blood through which we must enter to obtain salvation. Because of Christ's sacrifice, we are safe from the wrath of God that is going to be poured upon the world (1 Thess. 1:10; 5:9). This was Paul's comforting word to the church in spite of its troubles as it faced the case of the incestuous young man.

With this thought in mind, we must also consider Paul's comment in 1 Corinthians 5:5: ". . . that the spirit may be saved in the day of the Lord Jesus." This implies the rapture of the church detailed in 1 Thessalonians 4:13–18. Here the reference is to Christ who was sacrificed on our behalf as our Passover. He is our safety, sparing us from the Tribulation coming upon the world and described in Revelation chapters six through nineteen. An incident of an incestuous case cannot affect the ultimate survival of the church, even as Christ promised that the gates of hell shall not prevail against His church (Matt. 16:18).

LESSONS:

1. The Corinthian church not only failed to censure the young man involved in incestual sin, but also they were proud and boastful of their liberal tolerance toward him.
2. Instead of letting our sinful nature master us even for a short time, we are to respond to whatever blows the Holy Spirit give us to keep our sinful nature a slave.
3. The Christian Church is a fellowship of saints who hold their bodies in subjection.
4. Christ put down the old nature so that sin no longer prevails in us. He did not, however, eliminate the old nature, and we must continue to fight against it.

5. Paul confirms that the church consisted of believers who were unleavened, meaning without the prevalence of the sin nature in them, although some were spiritual babies and carnal.

1 Cor. 5:8 | Let Us Keep Celebrating—How and For What?

Therefore let us keep the feast, not with old leaven, neither with the leaven of malice and wickedness; but with the unleavened bread of sincerity and truth.

The scene described by Paul in the fifth chapter of First Corinthians has been a dismal one indeed. Almost everyone knew that a young man who was part of the Corinthian church was having an incestuous affair with his stepmother. Paul told the church they should put out this young man, deliver him to Satan for the destruction of his flesh that he may repent and be saved in the day of the Lord Jesus.

In 1 Corinthians 5:7 Paul reminded the church that its safety was based on Christ's sacrifice for it. And now in verse eight he goes on to tell the church that believers, in spite of difficulties experienced in the world and its infiltration into the church, ought to celebrate the eternal victory we have because of Christ and in Him. "Therefore let us keep [or celebrate] the feast." The significant thing is that this verb "celebrate" is used here only and nowhere else in the New Testament.

In the midst of sadness because of the inroad sin had made in the life of a particular individual and in the church, Paul gives a command that the church should celebrate in spite of his great concern. No matter what may overwhelm us, we must never lose sight that the church is on the victory side. Our victory, however, is in our Passover; our safety is in Christ Himself who became the Lamb who was sacrificed for us (v. 7). Our victory and celebration is based solely on that fact, and it is worth celebrating.

Our Joyful Celebration Is in Our Salvation

The mention of the day of the Lord Jesus in 1 Corinthians 5:5 is of paramount significance. Paul expressed the hope that the disciplinary action he was recommending to the church in Corinth was going to lead to rescuing the spirit of the incestuous young man. Note that emphasis is placed on such a rescue as implied by the verb "shall be saved" (*sōthḗ*) of verse five and also the preservation or the passing over implied in the word "passover" of verse seven.

Our lives as believers, in spite of all the adversities we experience, should show continuous celebration because of what Christ has done for us. Did you notice that little word "hope" in 1 Thessalonians 4:13 as Paul introduces so explicitly the rapture of the church? "But I would not have you [believers] to be ignorant, brethren, concerning them which are asleep [died], that you sorrow not, even as others [unbelievers] which have no hope." This hope that we as believers shall not experience the Great Tribulation (1 Thess. 1:10; 5:9) is a basic reason for our joy.

The verb *heortázōmen*, "let us keep the feast or celebrate," is in the present subjunctive and not in the aorist. It indicates that this feasting started when we believed on Christ who sacrificed Himself for us, and thus we never cease to celebrate. We are in a life of continuous celebration, for the joy of our salvation is unending.

But the most glorious celebration is yet to come as described in Hebrews 12:23: "To the general assembly [*panḗguris*, a festive convocation, a joyful assembly] and church of the firstborn, which are written in heaven, and to God the Judge of all, and to the spirit of just men made perfect [who have reached the goal set before them]." This is the ultimate feasting. It is interesting that believers here are called "the firstborn which are written in heaven." The Passover saved the Jewish firstborn. Jesus Christ the Paschal Lamb gave His life to effectively save all those who believe and they are called "the firstborn" as they partake of their ultimate heavenly celebration.

How Is this Continuous Celebration by Believers Achieved?

There are two negatives given: 1) "not with the old leaven" or by a return to our ways prior to our salvation; 2) "neither with the leaven of malice." "Malice" translates from the Greek word *kakía*. This, however, should be understood as inherent badness, evil, or depravity. It refers more to our character than our actions. After we are saved, the danger is to continue to be what we were before. If we were stubborn before our salvation, we continue to be stubborn, perhaps not in the same things of our former life, but we allow that stubbornness to carry over into our new life. For instance, in my new life I may learn a truth about a certain doctrine, but my old stubborn character may express itself when I insist upon that doctrine as if there were none other equally important or even more significant. I may even go so far as to convene certain gatherings to celebrate my ill-placed emphasis. Paul is teaching that we must not have such celebrations in the demonstration of our old sinful traits.

But then he goes on to add "and wickedness." This word is *ponēría*, "active evil, harmfulness." Depravity and evil are never restricted to privacy. They spill over into harmfulness. A stubborn, opinionated person is hardly ever satisfied in saying, "This is my opinion." He will do everything possible to make his opinion that of those with whom he comes in contact, and in the process he may do unspeakable harm to the whole cause of Christ. In the defense of what he considers truth, he may try to expose another's sins even though they may exist only in his imagination. His efforts may result far more in the defamation and blasphemy of the name and work of Christ than the correction of the erring brother.

These two traits, evil and harmfulness, are inseparable characteristics of the old leaven, and we must beware lest they are still affecting the whole dough.

Is it possible to separate any constituent part of kneaded dough? It has flour, leaven or yeast, water, salt, sugar, and butter. Can those ingredients be taken out of the dough after it has been kneaded and baked into bread? The individual ingredients in the dough and the bread lose their identity when they are mixed together and become a new element. Likewise, the Christian life is indeed a new creation (2 Cor. 5:17).[1] Such loss of that which characterized our former life is purely the work of the Holy Spirit, and as it is impossible to extract the elements that make up the dough or the bread, thus it is with the church of Christ. As the synthesis is the work of the Holy Spirit, so also is the analysis, the breaking up of what God put together. This young man, in allowing sin to take control of his life, could not break up the dough or lump. Paul now emphasizes that we should never celebrate the demonstration of what characterized our old leaven of depravity (*kakía*) and harmfulness (*ponēría*). The victory of the believer is not in shaming his brother, but the deliverance unto Satan for tasting the consequences of the sin of the flesh and for the reclamation of his spirit.

---

1. The Greek is *kainḗ ktísis: kainḗ,* "qualitatively new"; *ktísis,* "creation" or "creature."

Sincerity and Truth Need Not Be Dull Qualities in the Christian Life

There is a contrast between the new Christian life and the former sinful life. While the believer celebrates his redemption and salvation, the sinner celebrates his depravity and harmfulness. Self is his center, his pleasure is of the flesh. He boasts about how he pulled a fast one or beat someone in a fight or got to the top of the heap by stepping on others. He has a "dog-eat-dog" attitude, and since he believes that, he might as well be the one doing the eating.

Remember that in this case leaven is symbolic of sin. It raises the dough. It puffs one up in his sin. And the evil one who is called *ho ponērós*, "the harmful one," manages to persuade a person that as long as he can have a little fun and get ahead nothing else matters.

Let us celebrate not in the old leaven of sin and harmfulness, Paul says, "but with the unleavened bread of sincerity and truth."

"With the unleavened bread" translates from the Greek words *en azúmois*, which are not singular, but plural. There is no mention of bread at all. Actually it says "with what are unleavened" or "with unleavened qualities." Then Paul goes on to name those qualities, which are sincerity and truth.

Since leaven in this context stands for sin, we must take it to mean that our celebration or feasting in the Christian life must center on the sacrifice of Christ for us and never contain sinful elements. Pleasure is permissible for the believer, but not when it brings out our old nature which is selfish and harmful.

Godly feasting has two characteristics:

1) *It is sincere.*

The word for "sincerity" is *eilikríneia* and is found for the first time in the New Testament in 1 Corinthians 5:8. It means something that is not mixed. Bread contains leaven which in this context represents sin, and Paul says that what we celebrate should be free of sin. Wafers which have been prepared without yeast don't rise. They are flat. So sometimes to the nonbeliever our feastings seem "flat." "Wine, women and song" constitute fun for the nonbeliever, but a believer knows that feasting need not be sinful, if not accompanied by riotous and immoral acts.

2) *It is based on truth.*

In Philemon 1:18 "truth" (*alḗtheia*) stands as the opposite of pretense. If we pretend that we are in the truth while we enjoy sin all around us, we are not in the truth and our celebration or feasting will have leaven in it. The believer has enough in Christ's sacrifice to celebrate without any admixture of sinful practices.

LESSONS:

1. In 1 Corinthians 5:8 Paul tells the church that believers, in spite of the difficulties experienced in the world and its infiltration into the church, ought to celebrate the eternal victory they have because of Christ and in Him.
2. Because the verb *heortázōmen,* "let us keep the feast or celebrate," is in the present subjunctive and not in the aorist, it indicates that feasting started when we believed on Christ, and thus we never cease to celebrate.
3. There is a danger that after we are saved we will not only continue in our old sinful traits but that we will also have celebrations of them. Paul emphasizes that we should never celebrate the demonstration of what characterized our old leaven of depravity (*kakía*) and harmfulness (*ponēría*).
4. The believer delivers a sinning brother to Satan to taste the consequences of his fleshly sin in order to reclaim his spirit not to shame him.
5. Paul tells them to celebrate not in the old leaven of sin and harmfulness, "but with the unleavened bread of sincerity and truth."
6. The Greek word eilikríneia translated "sincerity" means something that is not mixed, whereas one finds in Philemon 1:18 that "truth" stands as the opposite of pretense.

1 Cor. 5:9

Watch the Company You Keep

I wrote unto you in an epistle not to company with fornicators.

Paul must have written another letter to the Corinthians besides the first and second epistles which we possess. We have no record of it. In the providence of God, it was not preserved for us, but this in no way should lead us to consider the Scriptures which we do possess as incomplete.

We do not possess a report of all the miracles the Lord Jesus did which His disciples witnessed (John 20:30), but what we have recorded is enough for the establishment and daily enactment of our faith. We must believe not only in the doctrine of inspiration (2 Tim. 3:16), but also in the ensuing doctrine of preservation. God's providence encompasses both. If we do not believe in the preservation of that which is necessary for doctrine and conduct, then we might assume that contradictions are contained in what has been lost. What we have in writing is sufficient that we may believe and through that belief have life (John 20:31).

When Paul told the Corinthian church, "I wrote unto you in an epistle," the definite article preceding "epistle" leads us to assume that he refers to a definitely known and different epistle.

The literal translation should be, "I wrote to you in the epistle." It could grammatically be assumed that he may be referring to this current epistle, but that is not likely since this is the first time that the admonition occurs in this epistle. In fact, this is the first time both the words *sunanamígnumi*, "to mix together with," and *pórnos*, "fornicator," occur. Thus we conclude that Paul could not refer to this epistle of Corinthians, since he has not thus far in this epistle discussed the subject itself.

The occasion of the well-publicized incest in the Corinthian church which Paul dealt with in verses one through eight leads him now to proffer some admonitions in conclusion.

The fact that he mentions a previous command not to mix with fornicators gives the advice more weight. In essence he is saying, "I am telling you again not to do it."

Sin among Believers and Nonbelievers

Before we discuss the verb *sunanamígnumi*, "to mix together with," it is necessary for us to discuss the noun *pórnois* (masc. pl. dat. of *pórnos*, "fornicator").

Corinth was a city characterized by immorality. On Acrocorinth, the top of a hill 1,800 feet above sea level, stood the temple of Aphrodite, the mythological goddess of love, fertility and beauty. She was said to have been born of the sea foam and was also the goddess of seafarers. Her temple had more than a thousand priestesses. They were called *hieródouloi*, "slaves or ministers of the temple." They were prostitutes (*pórnai*). The low moral standard prevailing in Corinth was such that the ministers of vice were called priestesses. Such were not found elsewhere in other shrines of Greece though they were common in the cities of Asia Minor. Corinth was thus frequented and enriched by the multitudes who resorted there to enjoy the pleasure of sin for a season. Immorality was so accepted in Corinth that there emerged a proverb that to live like a Corinthian (*Korinthiázesthai*) meant to live immorally. Such was the city when Paul preached and established a Christian church.

The noun *pórnos* and all that it characterized in Corinth was not applied to the incestuous man described in 1 Corinthians 5:1–8. His sin of having his father's wife is called *porneía*, "fornication" (1 Cor. 5:1), but throughout this chapter Paul does not call this incestuous young man a fornicator as such. In verse two he refers to him as "he that hath done this deed," but not "this fornicator." In verse three he speaks "concerning him that hath so done this deed." In verse five he says, "to deliver such a one unto Satan." Again, Paul does not call him a fornicator. It seems that perhaps Paul felt shame to even mention the word more than necessary, and perhaps he wanted to avoid mentioning the man's name.

Therefore, seeing how Paul refers to this young man who committed the sin of fornication but did not call him fornicator, we would do well to examine the word carefully.

A fornicator in Scripture is one who practices fornication as a way of life. Such cannot be a believer as is asserted in 1 John 3:6: "Whosoever abideth in him sinneth[1] [on a regular basis as a lifestyle] not; whosoever sinneth[2] [indicating again on a regular basis] hath not seen him neither known him." The verbs *heṓraken*, "has seen," and *égnōken*, "has known," are both in the perfect indicative, signifying that they never saw Him and never knew Him at any time and they do not see Him or know Him now.

To be a sinner may mean two things, one being that an individual never knew Christ as his Savior and Lord and needs that initial acquaintance with Jesus Christ to be saved. Jesus said

---

1.*Hamartánei,* the present indicative of *hamartánō,* "to sin."

2.*Ho hamartánon,* the present participle.

". . . I am not come to call the righteous, but sinners to repentance" (Matt. 9:13). These are the sinners who have never believed and become part of the body of Christ.

Paul, however, after his salvation uses the word in a different aspect and calls himself a sinner. "This is a faithful saying, and worthy of all acceptation, that Christ Jesus came into the world to save sinners, of whom I am [not merely I was] chief" (1 Tim. 1:15). It is possible for a believer to fall into sin (1 John 1:8–10; 2:1). He cannot be considered a sinner in the same category as the unsaved, but a sinner who cannot attain perfectly to the high and holy calling set before him.

When Paul advised the Corinthian church to deliver "such a one" to Satan, he was calling for his spirit to be saved from the power of such sin. The battle was between his fleshly desire and his spirit. And the meaning of "save," as we have already seen, indicates eschatological preservation in the day of the Lord Jesus. This did not have reference to his initial salvation which he evidently possessed.

Here the incestuous young man had fallen into the sin of fornication, but was not condemned by Paul as a fornicator. A fornicator in the New Testament was one whose lifestyle was that of repeated and continual sexual sin.

In verse ten Paul explains that he was speaking about "the fornicators of this world," that is the unsaved professional prostitutes.

In verse eleven he expands on the subject by saying that such a fornicator can only be called a brother because, in fact, he cannot be a real one.

In 1 Corinthians 6:9, 10 he assures us that "neither fornicators, nor idolaters, nor adulterers, nor effeminate, nor abusers of themselves with mankind [homosexuals], nor thieves, nor covetous, nor drunkards, nor revilers, nor extortioners, shall inherit the kingdom of God." These are all unsaved people. If they live in such a sinful lifestyle, they cannot be believers. This is why Paul in the eleventh verse says, "And such were some of you: but you are washed,[3] but you are sanctified,[4] but you are justified[5] in the name of the Lord Jesus, and by the Spirit of our God" [author's emphasis]. These verbs are all in the aorist passive voice which refers to what Christ did for such who were fornicators among them. These were not believers before their cleansing and sanctification.

A fornicator is never referred to even remotely as possibly being a believer. Every mention of a fornicator is accompanied with condemnation (see Eph. 5:5; 1 Tim. 1:10; Heb. 12:16; 13:4; Rev. 21:8; 22:15).

How Should Christians Treat Immoral Persons?

Paul does not specify as to which particular fornicators the believers in Corinth should avoid. There is no definite article before *pórnois*, "with fornicators," which indicates that it is dangerous for believers to keep company with those whose intention or desire is to lure them to prostitution or immorality. A true believer certainly is not comfortable or safe in the company of prostitutes.

This brings us to the necessity of examining the verb which is translated "to company." This verb *sunanamígnusthai* implies a closer connection than the synonymous preposition *metá*, "with." It implies not just a casual encounter but a joining together. The second word which helps form this verb is *aná*,

---

3.*Apeloúsasthe,* the aorist passive of *apoloúō,* "to wash fully," were fully washed.

4.*Hēgiásthēte,* the aorist passive of *hagiáxō,* "to make holy," for you were made holy.

5.*Edikaiṓthēte,* the aorist passive of *dikaióō,* "to justify," you were justified.

"on" or "upon," which in composition as a prefix implies repetition, increase, intensity. And the basic verb is *mígnumi*, "to mix, mingle." The meaning then of this triple compound verb is to be conjoined repeatedly to prostitutes. We can easily see that the Greek word has a stronger and more intense and intimate meaning than simply "to company." The active voice indicates a personal initiative to have repeated relationships with prostitutes. This is not company; it is throwing oneself into the fire. The advice is valid, and each one of us, no matter how good his standing in Christ, needs to take it seriously. Let us remember that the same apostle wrote to these Corinthian believers, "Wherefore let him that thinks he stands take heed lest he fall" (1 Cor. 10:12).

I well remember a young lady who came to me for counseling. Although she claimed to be a Christian, she immediately yielded to a sexual temptation that came her way. As she sat in our living room crying, I warned her to flee from evil and stay as far away from the young man as possible. Two weeks later, I heard that she had taken a job just across the street from where he worked. Her reasoning was that she wanted to prove to herself and God that she could resist the temptation. In no time at all, she was back into her sin. We cannot throw ourselves into sin's path and then expect God to deliver us.

The advice not to join oneself repeatedly with prostitutes was not something which Paul wrote in a previous epistle and now tries to correct as being too strict. Rather, he is reaffirming it, for in 1 Corinthians 5:11 he writes, "But now I have written unto you not to keep company [*sun-anamígnusthai*, exactly the same verb], if any man that is called a brother be a fornicator. . . , with such a one, no, not to eat." The particle *dé* translated "but" should be translated "and." Thus the verse would read "And now. . . ," that is, what I said previously I repeat here and now.

Besides 1 Corinthians 5 verses 9 and 11 where the infinitive *sunanamígnusthai* occurs, it is also used in 2 Thessalonians 3:14 where Paul says, "And if any man obey not our word by this epistle, note that man, and have no company [*sunanamígnusthai*] with him, that he may be ashamed." Here Paul speaks of those who walk in a disorderly manner, not wanting to work. Do not associate with such a person, Paul admonishes. He will affect your work ethic.

Immoral sex and laziness are to be shunned. In the case of this lazy man, he is a brother, and Paul concludes his admonition by saying, "Yet count him not as an enemy, but admonish him as a brother."

LESSONS:

1. Not only has Paul given a previous command to not mix together with fornicators, but also in conclusion to the well-publicized incest in the Corinthian church he is lead to say in essence, "I am telling you again not to do it."
2. Because of the wide acceptance of immorality in Corinth, there emerged a proverb stating that to live like a Corinthian meant to live immorally.
3. Since Paul refers to the young man who committed fornication without calling him fornicator, we ought to study what the term fornicator means.
4. According to the Scripture a fornicator practices fornication as a way of life and is thus an unbeliever (1 John 3:6).
5. Paul tells the Corinthians to "not company" with fornicators. By studying the Greek one finds that the active voice given here indicates that "to company" indicates a personal initiative to have repeated relationships with prostitutes.

1 Cor. 5:10 Do Not Be an Isolationist

Yet not altogether with the fornicators of this world, or with the covetous, or extortioners, or with idolaters; for then must ye needs go out of the world.

The verb "to company" in verse nine is to be understood in the context of verse ten: "And not at all to company. . . ." This is not a negation of what Paul stated in his "previous" epistle to the Corinthians referred to in verse nine, but rather a confirmation and explanation. The negative "not" in verse nine is *mḗ*, which implies a dependent and conditional subjective negative. Verse nine uses the "not" subjectively. Its message is this: There are prostitutes in the world. You cannot eliminate their presence, but subjectively you do not have to conjoin yourself to them. While they may be present, keep yourself pure by not mixing together with them (see 1 Tim. 5:22; 2 Tim. 2:22).

The verb *sunanamígnusthai*, "to mix closely together," although it does not appear in verse ten, is to be understood as implied after *ou*, "not at all." The command is "and not at all to mix intimately in any way with the prostitues of this world." In fact, the "not" in verse ten is the more absolute objective *ou*. Paul makes his admonition of verse nine clear. The way not to get involved with prostitutes is not to mix up in any way with them.

But what does the adverb *pántōs* mean? It occurs only nine times in the New Testament, and five of the nine times it is used by Paul (Rom. 3:9; 1 Cor. 5:10; 9:10, 22; 16:12). Only twice, in 1 Corinthians 5:10 and Romans 3:9, is it used with the negative *ou*, "not," as *ou pántōs*, where it is translated "no, in no wise." Here also the verb preceding is implied. Romans 3:9 says, "are we better than they?" The Greek verb is *proechómetha* as a question, meaning "do we excel?" The answer is *ou*, "not," that is, we do not excel, and then *pántōs*, "in no way." It is an affirmation that absolutely we do not excel.

In the same way, the *ou pántōs* must be understood in 1 Corinthians 5:10 as relating to verse nine: "I wrote unto you in an epistle not to company [have close repeated relations] with fornicators." Then verse ten should be translated: "No, indeed, not in any way should we have close repeated relations with. . . ." Then Paul defined what he meant by fornicators and adds a few more unsavory characters to "the fornicators of this world." Paul is not speaking of the church, because in the true church of Jesus Christ there are no fornicators. Although he had just spoken about a man who fell into fornication, the man was not a fornicator as such. This class of people all belong to the world. They are of the world and in the world.

Which People Must We Avoid?

But let us examine these other morally offensive characters whom we are to avoid. The first is covetous people. The word is *pleonéktēs* and refers to one who always wants to have more and will do anything he can to defraud others to achieve gain. In every passage of Scripture where the word *pleonéktēs*, "a covetous or greedy person," occurs, it is always in a list with *pórnos*, "fornicator." This greed must be conceived not only in the realm of material goods, but also in the area of lust. We find this in Ephesians 4:19: "Who being past feeling have given themselves over unto lasciviousness, to work all uncleanness with greediness." It is the same word *pleonexía*, the noun of *pleonéktēs*. It can also refer to malicious slander which robs another of his honor.

He who is greedy will resort to extortion to gain what he wants. So Paul adds extortioners to the list. The Greek word is *hárpax*. It is a rapacious person, one who attacks suddenly in order to steal, one who preys on others.

Another person in the world that we are admonished to stay away from is the idolater (*eidōlolátrēs*, "idol worshiper"). In fact, not only are we told that in no way should we intimately mix with such people, but we are also told to flee or run away (*pheúgō*, "to run away") from the practices which constitute their way of life:

1 Corinthians 6:18: "Flee fornication. . . ."

1 Corinthians 10:14: ". . . flee idolatry."

2 Timothy 2:22: "Flee also youthful lusts."

Flee from the vices, and avoid the perpetrators of such sins. They are out to trip you up.

Must We Withdraw from the World to Live a Separated Life?

What are we as Christians then to do? Leave the world? No, this is an impossibility. Our Lord's high-priestly prayer was, "I pray not that thou should take them out of the world, but that thou should keep them from the evil" (John 17:15).

Paul concludes, "For then you must needs go out of the world." What is translated "for then" in Greek is *epeí* from *epí*, "upon which case," and *ei*, "if," a conjunction expressing a condition which is purely hypothetical and separate from all experience, meaning "for if in such a case"; "then" translates *ára*, used interrogatively which requires a negative answer. The question therefore is, "If that were so, would it not be necessary for you to leave the world?" The verb for "be necessary" is *opheílete*, the present indicative of *opheílō*, "ought to." This is the reading in the Textus Receptus and hence the KJV is perfectly fitting: "for then you must needs go out of the world." Thus, the obvious answer is, "If that were so, in order to live as a victorious believer, you would have to leave the world."

The conclusion is that we as believers need not go out of the world in order to avoid close relationships with the unsaved around us in order that we may have victory. We can be in the world, and yet not of it. We are to influence it for good, but not intimately mix with it and allow it to seduce us. We must realize that hardened and professional sinners such as prostitutes, extortioners, idolaters, or the avaricious are dedicated to their evil, and close company with them will soon contaminate us.

Monasticism is not the solution to our interaction with the world. Whereas we cannot avoid the presence of sinners, we must exercise caution and soberness. The word that should guide the Christian in the world is *sōphrosúnē*, "soundness of mind," or common sense or wisdom. It will guide as to how far we should stay away from the forces which can consume us, and at the same time help us to realize that we are the recipients of God's gifts for more than overcoming the world (Rom. 8:37).

The Limits of Our Freedom

In 2 Timothy 1:7 we read, "For God has not given us the spirit of fear; but of power, and of love, and of a sound mind." The word for a "sound mind" is *sōphrosúnē*. It prescribes the limits of our freedom in the world. It tells us how close we may get to those whose desire is to beguile us. The word "fear" in this verse is not the word *phóbos*, "scare," but *deilía*, "timidity." When prostitutes, covetous people, extortioners, and idolaters are all around us, we cannot go and hide in a monastery. This is what the verb *exeltheín*,[1] "to go out of," in 1 Corinthians 5:10 implies. The overwhelming presence of sin does not cause us to withdraw to a protected haven, but to "run with patience the race that is set before us" (Heb. 12:1).

Then, as Paul said to Timothy, God's gift of power enabling us to stand our ground in victory and witness will follow. In addition He puts love in our hearts for those whose intentions and influences we realize and avoid. "Love" here is not lust, but *agápē*. It is a passion for sharing what we have and what others need, the Lord Jesus Christ. What a marvelous gift God has given us to be able to live victoriously in a world which tries so hard to win us over.

What more could we want than to be able to stand strong and yet be loving, to have a wise and sound mind?

LESSONS:

1. First Corinthians 5:10 is a confirmation and explanation of verse 9.
2. Since the presence of prostitutes cannot be eliminated from the world, keep yourself pure by not mixing together with them.
3. Not only are we told not to intimately mix with prostitues, but we are also told to flee or run away (*pheúgō*) from the practices which constitute their way of life.
4. Not only does God give us the power to enable us to live victoriously in a world trying to win us over to sin, but he also puts love in our hearts for those trying to beguile us.

1.The aorist infinitive of *exérchomai*.

1 Cor. 5:11 | *Beware of False Christians*

But now I have written unto you not to keep company, if any man that is called a brother be a fornicator, or covetous, or an idolater, or a railer, or a drunkard, or an extortioner; with such a one, no, not to eat.

The first thing that we must understand as we read this admonition of Paul concerning our social restrictions as Christians in the world is the verb translated "to keep company." It is the same verb as found in verse nine, *sunanamígnusthai*,[1] "to mix closely together." It does not mean to isolate oneself from those people completely, but rather to avoid their close and repeated company. Such people spell danger to the Christian. Whatever contact the believer has, he should keep his eyes open and not be drawn into their way of life.

Purity in the midst of the filth that prevails in the world is entirely possible. Paul would not otherwise have advised Timothy to keep himself pure (1 Tim. 5:22). The adjective Paul uses is *agnós*, "chaste," referring to moral purity (see also 2 Cor. 11:2; 1 Pet. 3:2). Nature itself teaches us this. What beautiful flowers, unspotted and unsoiled, grow up out of the dirt of the earth.

1.The present infinitive of *sunanamígnumi*, "to mix up, closely and repeatedly.

In Titus 2:5 where the word *agnós* occurs in relation to the desired behavior of young women, it is preceded by the adjective *sō̆phronas*, "discreet, of sound mind," and thus voluntarily limiting their own freedom. When young women can voluntarily limit their freedom, they will be chaste.

James in his epistle goes a step further insofar as how little the world can influence the believer who determines to stay pure. He says ". . . and to keep himself unspotted from the world" (James 1:27). The word for "unspotted" is *áspilos*. This refers to moral spots, of course. There is a protective element surrounding the Christian which can keep him from the immoral dirt prevailing all over the world. But this moral "teflon" is not automatically applied. It is to be put on. Observe the verb "to keep himself unspotted." It is possible, but the closer something clean comes to something unclean, the more likely it is to become soiled.

Paul did not change his admonition about believers not having intimate relations with fornicators. He wrote this in a former epistle as he stated in verse nine. It is difficult to reconcile the word "now" (*nunî*) with the aorist verb *égrapsa*, "I wrote." How can Paul say "now" I wrote to you? The adverb *nuní* sometimes is used as a particle of transition, as if saying, "I wrote to you, and now I am still writing the same thing to you. This principle I enunciated to you still holds true." The verb "to keep company" is the same *sunanamígnusthai* as in verse nine.

Sinners Do Penetrate the Church

But now Paul delineates the possibility of the sinners he described in verse ten being not only in the world, but as having also penetrated the church. And they are not only in the church, they are also called "brothers."

If someone is called a "brother," but is a fornicator, a covetous individual, an idolater, or an extortioner, he is certainly not a brother. What Paul is intimating is that we may expect to find such people who have joined the church, but they are not real brothers. They are only called such because they are giving a false impression. In fact, they may be more dangerous within the church where they may be deceiving true believers.

To these unsavory characters Paul adds two more, a railer and a drunkard. The "railer" in Greek is *loídoros*, "a reviler." This adjectival noun occurs only twice here and in 1 Corinthians 6:10. In both passages, it is listed among sinners of the worst kind who are not going to inherit the kingdom of God. It describes a deceiver as one who beguiles others to believe his malicious false charges or misrepresentations intended to damage another's reputation. The reason why Paul included such a defamer and blasphemer in the ranks of those who parade in the church as so-called brothers is that they specialize in ruining the reputation of other genuine Christians within the church. The world does not particularly occupy itself in defaming believers. The world leaves that to their spiritual brothers. And there are many within the church who do much harm by engaging in such defamation.

The other kind of individual included in verse eleven, but not in verse ten, is a "drunkard," *méthusos*, which occurs only here and in 1 Corinthians 6:10. Intoxication is not to be taken lightly. Scripture condemns it repeatedly.

How Close Can We Be to Unbelievers?

The apostle then admonishes true believers not even to eat with such sinners. The verb *sunesthíein* is the present infinitve of *sunesthíō* which derives from the preposition *sún*, "with," and implies a closer connection and conjunction than the synonymous preposition *metá*, "with." The same preposition is used in the compound verb *sunanamígnumi* used in verses 9, 11. The verb *sunesthíō*, used here, means more than casually eating together. It indicates approval of the practices of the person you eat with.

In Luke 15:1 we read, "Then drew near unto him [Jesus] all the publicans and sinners for to hear him." The Pharisees and scribes took advantage of this as an occasion to attack Him by saying, "This man receiveth sinners, and eateth with them" (Luke 15:2). The word for "eateth with" is the same verb as in 1 Corinthians 5:11, *sunesthíō*, implying approval of their way of life.

"And when Peter was come up to Jerusalem, those who were of the circumcision contended with him, saying, you went in to men uncircumcised, and did eat with them" (Acts 11:2, 3). The same word *sunesthíō* is used. They accused him of identifying with their philosophy of life.

Likewise, in Galatians 2:12 Peter is accused by Paul of eating together with the Gentiles; that is, he lived like a Gentile in spite of the fact that he himself was a Jew.

Is Paul's recommendation to the Corinthian believers contrary to Christ's direction in regard to their behavior toward others? Did He not teach that we should love our enemies (Matt. 5:44)? Yes, indeed. To love them is expressed with the verb *agapáō* which means to discern their need and to share with them what we have and they lack, which is, of course, Jesus Christ. The Lord never commanded us to befriend them, which would have been expressed with the verb *philéo.*

James advises against the initiative of believers to befriend the world. He says, "You adulterers and adulteresses, know you not that the friendship of the world is enmity with God? Whosoever therefore will be a friend of the world is the enemy of God" (James 4:4).

Paul wanted the Corinthian believers to recognize that there are certain people from whom we must protect ourselves because of their aggressive evil intent. We should shun them and not mix with them intimately and repeatedly. We are not to invite them into our houses to eat with us thus exposing ourselves to temptation and the appearance of evil. This will bring dishonor to the name of Christ.

Stay Far Away from Those Trying to Deceive You

A danger exists from those who profess to be our brothers in Christ but are still sinners trying to entice us. Such were the ones described in 2 Peter 2:13: "And shall receive the reward of unrighteousness, as they that count it pleasure to riot in the daytime. Spots they are and blemishes, sporting themselves with their own deceivings while they feast with you." They were not only false brothers, pretenders, but even false teachers. Let us examine this verse carefully from the Greek text:

They bring upon themselves the retribution of unrighteousness (*komioúmenoi* is the pres. part. pass. mid. of the verb *komízō*, "to bring"; *misthón*, "retribution"; *adikías*, "unrighteousness").

They consider it a pleasure as they live in riotous luxury during the daytime. They "live it up." The words used are *hēdonḗ*, "lust, pleasure," from which the English word "hedonism" derives, and *truphḗ*, "luxury, debauchery." Their luxury even during the daytime is similar to nightclub life.

They are stains, dirty ones. This word is *spíloi*, "visibly dirty ones." Anyone who touches them gets dirty, too.

They are morally blameworthy. This word is *mṓmoi*, "moral stains, disgraces." Any association with them implies moral blame.

They live in luxury. *Entruphṓntes* is the present participle of *eutrupháō*, "to live in luxury." (The noun *truphḗ* in this verb is related to this verb also.)

They have deceived themselves, and they deceive others. *Apátais* is the dative plural of *apátē*, "deceit," both passively and actively. They have been deceived by those whose mere profession of faith caused them to be accepted as believers. And while they may live in unbelievable sin, they mislead others asking them to follow them.

They are doing this while they are feasting with you. The word is *suneuōchoúmenoi*, the present middle of *suneuōchéō*, meaning "to feast together." The verb is derived in part from the preposition *sún*, "together," implying conjoining, a close connection. This is the same prepositional prefix of the two important and basic verbs in this fifth chapter of 1 Corinthians: *sunanamígnumi*, "to repeatedly and closely mix together" in verse nine and *sunesthíō*, "to eat together" implying identification of philosophy of life in verse eleven. The other words which make up *suneuōchéō* are *eu*, "good, well," and *échō*, "to have." Thus *euōchéō* means to have a good time. The verb *suneuōchéomai* means to have a good time of feasting with others. It is also used in a similar way in Jude 1:12.

When it comes to the proselytizers of false doctrines, the advice of the apostle John is even more strict. His advice is that we should not even greet them. "If there come any unto you, and bring not this doctrine, receive him not into your house, neither bid him Godspeed, for he that biddeth him Godspeed is partaker of his evil deeds" (2 John 1:10, 11).

LESSONS:

1. Purity is possible in the midst of the prevailing filth in the world.
2. The closer something clean comes to something unclean, the more likely it is to become soiled.
3. The apostle admonishes true believers not even to eat with the false believers found within the church who are fornicators, drunkards.
4. The verb *sunesthíō* does not merely mean casually eating together but rather indicates an approval of the practices of the person you eat with.

1 Cor. 5:12, 13 — *Who Will Judge Whom?*

For what have I to do to judge them also that are without? do not ye judge them that are within? But them that are without God judgeth. Therefore put away from among yourselves that wicked person.

We must remember that in verse three Paul stated his own conviction that this young man was indeed guilty of immorality. "For I verily, as absent in body, but present in spirit, have judged already, as though I were present, concerning him that has so done this deed."

Paul must have examined the evidence although we have no indication as to how or for how long. This is a requirement for any of us as individuals to do before we make a decision as to whether necessary discipline should be applied to an individual.

The verb Paul uses is *kékrika*[1] which in this instance means to make one's personal evaluation on a matter. It is not a judgment of the whole life of this young man or his family, but of a particular deed or sinful lifestyle as it developed. Observe how Paul expresses it: "I . . . have judged . . . concerning him that has so done this deed." If you ever receive a letter about a brother and

---

1. The perfect of *krínō*.

the writer finds fault with every aspect of the accused to prove that he is no good at all, the best thing to do is to disregard it. Our courts of justice today will not examine the whole life of an individual, but will sit in judgment only on a specific deed or deeds and determine whether those particular allegations are true or false. The past criminal record of a person cannot be introduced as evidence in a case if a person has served his sentence for these crimes. Total condemnation of a person is the type of judgment which Scripture forbids whether the person concerned is a believer or an unbeliever. We are not the judges over our fellow human beings, be they believers or unbelievers.

What confronted Paul and the Corinthian church was an internal matter. The fact that the church failed to act to discipline the incestuous man was considered wrong by Paul. His recommendation was that the man should be expelled from the fellowship of the church and delivered to Satan to experience the painful consequences of succumbing to evil, namely, the physical destruction of moral perversion. Also, the pain of cutting him off from the church should help him turn from his sinful state. That is as far as Paul instructed any personal judgment and church discipline to go.

Those Who Are Without

But now in verse twelve he asks, "What, is it mine to judge also those outside?" As an apostle, he felt he had a responsibility toward those within the church, especially the Corinthian church that he had an active part in establishing (Acts 18:1–17), for in First Corinthians 4:14 he calls them his beloved children (cf. 2 Cor. 6:13).

Christians must realize that they are not of the world. There is a wall of separation which is Christ—built between the world and the church. "Have you not made a hedge about him, and about his house, and about all that he has on every side?" (Job

1:10). Thus we have those who are outside and those who are inside. The separation was introduced by the Lord Jesus Himself as He explained the purpose of His parables. He said to His disciples ". . . unto you it is given to know the mystery of the kingdom of God: but unto them that are without, all these things are done in parables" (Mark 4:11).

Paul also called those in the world "those without." In Colossians 4:5 he wrote: "Walk in wisdom toward them that are without, redeeming the time." And in 1 Thessalonians 4:12 he wrote: "That you may walk honestly toward them that are without, and that you may have lack of nothing." In 1 Timothy 3:7 he says of a bishop that "he must have a good report of them which are without; lest he fall into reproach and the snare of the devil." In Revelation 22:15 we read, "For without are dogs, and sorcerers, and whoremongers, and murderers, and idolaters, and whosoever loves and makes a lie."

Thus Paul, more than any spiritual leader in the Scriptures, recognizes those who are without, in the world, and those who are within, in the church or in Christ. The church has its own pattern of behavior which is distinct from that of the world.

"To judge" in Greek is *kríno* which has a variety of meanings determined by the context. Essentially it means to separate, distinguish, discriminate between good and evil, to form or give an opinion after separating and considering the particulars of a case.

Believers cannot help but come to the opinion that those who are characterized by the works of the flesh are outside of Christ. These works are specified as manifest, open, easily detectable (see Gal. 5:19–21). They are adultery, fornication, uncleanness, lasciviousness or an insatiable appetite for sensual pleasure (*asélgeia*). Observe that these first four pertain to sexual sins. Then follows idolatry which is allowing anything other than God to be the center of one's life. Other demonstrations of being controlled by the evil one are "witchcraft, hatred, contention, jealousies, anger, self-seeking rivalry, divisions, heresies, envyings, murders, drunkenness, revelings and such like . . . they which do such things shall not inherit the kingdom of God [a.t.]" (Gal. 5:20, 21).

A Pastor's First Duty Is to His Own Church

The apostle Paul knew that those in the world did not need merely correction of their actions by him, but they needed to be evangelized and born-again. The world institutes its own authority which, under God's sovereignty, is set over unbelievers and believers alike (Rom. 13:1). Government is the regulator of law and order (Rom. 13:4). By saying, "What am I also to judge those on the outside?" Paul asserts that he is not to do the work of the secular government or the police. He has enough to do with the care of the churches of Christ. In 2 Corinthians 11:28 after enumerating his sufferings and persecutions from those without and false brethren within, he concludes: "Beside those things that are without, that which comes upon me daily, the care of all the churches." The word for "care" in Greek is *hēmérimna* which refers to extreme care and concern which becomes worry. In essence Paul is saying in 1 Corinthians 5:12, "I have enough worry discerning the behavior of those within the church as to whether it is becoming to the teaching of Christ." Such concern was an apostolic preoccupation, and by extension it ought to be that of every minister of a local congregation. But if a minister preoccupies himself with the sins of the world per se, he will not have enough time and strength to watch over his flock. A local pastor in the New Testament is called *epískopos*, "bishop, superintendent"; it is one who watches in a concerned way.

The Final Judgment

The word "judge" in 1 Corinthians 5:12 refers to the judgment which Scripture declares is going to come at the end upon the sons of disobedience (see Eph. 5:6). Jesus Christ is going to bring that about in due time at the consummation of the age. Until such time, however, it is God's will that the world not be condemned prematurely, but that the world through Jesus Christ might be saved (see John 3:17). The Father "has entrusted all judgment to the Son" (John 5:22). This prerogative of eschatological judgment has never been given to any apostle. Salvation is open to all, but those who reject it are condemned already (see John 3:18, 19).

The apostle Paul does not and cannot claim participation or determination in this final eschatological judgment either of believers or unbelievers. The Lord Jesus is the only judge of this. "Marvel not at this," Jesus said, "For the hour is coming, in which all that are in the graves shall hear his voice, and shall come forth; they that have done good unto the resurrection of life; and they that have done evil, unto the resurrection of damnation" (John 5:28, 29).

It is to this final judgment that Paul refers in 1 Corinthians 5:13 when he says, "But them that are without God judgeth. . . ." Some translations follow the UBS text which places the accent on the ultima instead of the penult: *krineí*, "will judge," instead of *krínei*, "he judges." Since accents were not used in ancient manuscripts, we cannot categorically say which is correct. Seeing that our present judgment by God revolves around our own decision to believe or not believe, if this verb were to be taken as the present tense, it would preempt the possibility of a last breath repentance and salvation. Such a last moment salvation can be found in the case of the repentant thief on the cross to whom Jesus said, "Verily, I say unto you, today you shall be with me in with me in paradise" (Luke 23:43). It is for this reason that I consider this verb to be in the future tense. "For them that are without, God will judge." This presupposes that such would die in unbelief for "... it is appointed unto men once to die, but after this the judgment [*krísis*, the subst. of the verb *krínō*, used in 1 Cor. 5:12, 13]." This is the eschatological or final judgment. In the explanation of the Parable of the Wheat and the Tares, the Lord Jesus makes it amply clear that He Himself never capriciously cuts the cord of opportunity for anyone to believe and be saved. Only in the case of Judas did He make an exception in the exercise of His omniscience (John 13:26, 27). If even Jesus Christ withheld such judgment, neither may we prejudge anyone to perdition (Matt. 13:36–43).

How Are We to Judge Our Fellow Believers in a Local Church?

Any flippant reader of the New Testament would find unjustified fault in it as contradicting itself. For example, consider the words of Christ in Matthew 7:1, 2, "Judge not that you be not judged, for with what judgment you judge, you shall be judged: and with what measure you mete, it shall be measured to you again." On the other hand the apostle Paul chides the Corinthian believers, ". . . do not you judge them that are within?" which refers, of course, to those in the church fellowship. He speaks to them implying it was their duty to judge those within the local church.

This is a negative question in which the negative adverb *ouchí* is used. *Ouchí* is a strengthened form of the negative particle *ou*, "not," which implies direct and full negation, independently and absolutely. Paul might have said, "Why on earth did you not make an objective evaluation of the situation in question and promptly arrive at the proper course of action?" The answer to such a question is expected to be positive, for this is a matter in which believers of a local church ought to judge and act.[2] The verb is the same as that used in Matthew 7:1, 2. Is Paul, therefore, contradicting the Lord who said "judge not"?

In Matthew 7:1, 2 we have a general principle of our Lord not to judge the character of a brother while we ourselves have our own weaknesses to discern and correct. The Lord Jesus is addressing a hypocrite.[3] A general negative attitude toward our fellow believers is sufficient proof of our own hypocrisy. Our judgment is usually according to appearances, hence not a righteous judgment (John 7:24). No matter how perfect a person may be, there are some who can find fault with him. As a human being, our Lord ate and drank to sustain His physical body as we all do, and yet there were those who accused Him of being a glutton and a winebibber (Matt. 11:19; Luke 7:34). He could not please them all, nor did He try, and He said we should not try to either. In fact, He pronounced woe unto us if we do so that everybody may pat us on the back (Luke 6:26).

Evaluation Versus Condemnation

The judgment referred to in Matthew 7:1, 2 is explained in Luke 6:37 as referring not to mere evaluation but to condemnation based on the appearance of a situation. "Judge not, and you shall not be judged: condemn not, and you shall not be condemned: forgive, and you shall be forgiven" (Luke 6:37). To find fault in another for the purpose of condemning him is improper.

Condemnation was not the motive of Paul when he said about the incestuous young man in 1 Corinthians 5:3: "I have already judged him." His discovery of the young man's sin never

---

2.See futher uses of such "why not" questions in Matt. 5:46; 20:13; Luke 12:6; 17:17; John 11:9; Rom. 3:29.

3.*Hypokritēs* or one who pretends perfection as in Matt. 7:5.

motivated Paul to speak of him with hopelessness. On the contrary, he said to the Corinthian church that they should "deliver such a one unto Satan for the destruction of the flesh, that the spirit may be saved in the day of the Lord Jesus" (1 Cor. 5:5). Paul's judgment of him was not condemnatory of his character; rather it was an indepth evaluation and verification of his sin. Upon verification, every prayerful endeavor toward his repentance and reclamation to Christ and the fellowship of believers was to be made. Paul did not dig into the life of this young man to enumerate and exaggerate on his other weaknesses. Can we be naïve enough to think he did not have such? Paul did not take a moral inventory of the young man but sought to redemptively address the sin he had observed. To do anything more and to recommend any other course to the church in the matter would have been wrong.

The verb that Paul uses in 1 Corinthians 5:12, 13 is *krínō*, "to judge," and should not be taken to mean condemnation. Basically it means to form an opinion after separating and considering the particulars in the case. It is to evaluate and determine what is right, proper, and expedient for correction. It stands opposite to paying no attention and sweeping the scandal under the rug. Whatever happens in the local church affects not only those who constitute the local church, but the church universal. As believers, our responsibility to the world is to reach them with the gospel of Christ. That is the basic need of every unbeliever, not merely to have this or the other shortcoming in his or her conduct corrected.

Paul gives sound advice to the Thessalonian believers: "Prove all things; hold fast that which is good" (1 Thess. 5:21). The believer is to differentiate as Paul suggests in Romans 16:17: "Now I beseech you, brethren, mark them which cause divisions and offenses [scandals] contrary to the doctrine which you have learned; and avoid them." That is judging things and people. Do not judge to condemn, but to correct and protect yourselves and the local church.

The verb *krínō*, "to judge," must be distinguished from two other Greek words. The first is *katakríno*, "to condemn," derived from *katá*, "down, against," and *krínō*, "to judge." In Romans 2:1 we have both of these words used: "Therefore you are inexcusable, O man, whosoever you are that judges [*krínō*] another, you condemn [*katakrínō*] yourself; for you that judge do the same thing." The understanding of this verse lies in the proper rendering of what is translated "another" (*héteros*). It is another who is different than you are. If the only reason you judge another person is because he is different than you are, the basis of your judgment is faulty; and no wonder you will condemn him, for, after all, who is better than self! Only God knows the extent of suffering there has been in this world because people have judged their fellowmen by the color of their skin or the slant of their eyes. Undoubtedly much of the warring and rioting and bloodshed in the world today is due to just such judgment.

The other word is *katadikáízō*, "to condemn": "Ye have condemned and killed [*phoneúō*, to murder] the just . . ." (James 5:6; cf. Matt. 12:7, 37; Luke 6:37).

Thus Paul chides the believers in Corinth for not judging or discerning the situation in order to redeem the incestuous young man. But he did not want them to condemn him or destroy him before trying to reconcile him again to Christ.

How Will God Judge Unbelievers?

Those that are without are unbelievers and those that are within (v. 12) are the church. God is the ultimate judge of all through Jesus Christ. "For we must all appear before the judgment seat of Christ; that every one may receive the things done in his body, according to what he has done, whether it be good or bad" (2 Cor. 5:10).

Specifically about unbelievers, Paul asks, "... Do you think you will escape the judgment of God?" Then he continues: "... after your hardness and impenitent heart, you treasure up unto yourself wrath against the day of wrath and revelation of the righteous judgment of God, who will render to every man according to his deeds" (Rom. 2:3, 5, 6).

Of the final destiny of the wicked we read, "... they are the enemies of the cross of Christ, whose end is destruction" (Phil. 3:18, 19). The word translated "destruction" is *apṓleia*, "lostness." It is the destiny of ungodly people. Second Peter 3:7 asserts that ungodly men are reserved unto fire against the day of judgment[3] and perdition.[4] Perdition is the eternal lost condition or separation from God, the second death (Rev. 2:11; 20:6, 14; 21:8).

Paul declares physical death, the separation of the soul from the body, to be God's punishment for man's sin (Rom. 5:12, 14; 1 Cor. 15:24ff). Prior to physical death which is common to unbelievers and believers alike is the spiritual death which is man's spiritual separation from God (see Eph. 2:1). The immediate result of the exercise of genuine faith by man is spiritual salvation (see Rom. 8:23), but only at the believer's resurrection is the redemption of the body experienced. As believers we do not exactly know what we shall yet be (see 1 John 3:1, 2). We do know, however, that we shall be like Him and shall be with the Lord forever (1 Thess. 4:13–18). Our bodies as believers will be imperishable, glorious, and spiritual.

What a believer receives when he believes is eternal life (see John 3:16). This is the life of God in the believer which the unbeliever does not have. He is dead in his sins, separated from

---

3.*Krísis,* the noun of *krínō,* "to judge."

4.*Apṓleia,* "lostness or perdition."

God. He is outside not only of the fellowship of the church, but also estranged from God. When believers and unbelievers die, they continue as they were in their earthly state insofar as their relationship to God or the absence of it is concerned (see Luke 16:19–31). Although the term "eternal life" is used frequently in the New Testament, the term "eternal death" never occurs. Instead, the New Testament uses the term *apṓleia*, "loss, perdition," which is rendered "destruction" in Matthew 7:13. This word *apṓleia*, "perdition," is used as a synonym of "eternal fire" in Matthew 18:8, "eternal punishment" in Matthew 25:4, 6, or "the second death" in Revelation 21:8. That this destiny awaits unbelievers is clearly stated in Revelation 21:8: "But the fearful, and unbelieving and the abominable and murderers, and whoremongers [*pórnoi*, "fornicators"], and sorcerers, and idolaters, and all liars, shall have their part in the lake which burns with fire and brimstone; which is the second death."

In Revelation 22:15 such unrepentant sinners are said to be "without" (*éxō*), the same as the unbelievers who are designated as those "without" in 1 Corinthians 5:12, 13. These are outside the church now and they will be outside of heaven where the believers will be with Christ (Acts 1:11; Phil. 1:23). Among the unbelievers who are without are not only those who pay no attention to the gospel, but also false prophets and teachers who may have been miracle workers according to Matthew 7:21–23. They will beg to come into the kingdom of heaven but will not be admitted.

The final destiny of unbelievers is the "lake of fire burning with brimstone" (Rev. 19:20) where the Antichrist and the false prophet are cast (see Rev. 19:20; 20:10, 15), as well as the devil and "whosoever was not found written in the book of life."

The Lord Jesus clearly told us that this lake of fire is a place of final punishment and was prepared for the devil and his angels (see Matt. 25:41). This was, therefore, not part of God's original creation, but it must have been created after Satan's fall as described in Isaiah 14:12–23. Since those who are without the church which is Christ's body (see Eph. 1:23; 1 Cor. 12:13) have elected to follow Satan, it is only natural that their destiny be the same as that of him and his angels.

How Should a Misbehaving Member of a Church Be Treated?

What should we do if we discover that a member of a Christian church who is thought to be in good standing is involved in illicit sexual relationships, participating in business practices that can hardly be distinguished from stealing or extortion, or otherwise engaging himself in some public sin? What is the church's duty toward such a person and toward the maintenance of the integrity of the church?

The end of verse five is a command: ". . . Therefore put away from among yourselves that wicked person." There is a variety of readings of the verb *exaírō*, "put away," as to the mood in which it is found. The Textus Receptus from which the KJV is translated has *exareíte* which is the future indicative active meaning "you shall remove him." It has the force of a command as if it were an imperative implying a particular person in question. The UBS text has *exárate*, the aorist imperative active which is a command. This word differs from *exareíte* in that it refers more to the authority of the one giving the command than the certainty of its being carried out. And finally a third reading is *exaírete* which is the present indicative with the force of command being on a permanent basis as if it were a principle established as a result of this particular case. It is this last reading that is preferable. Here Paul closes with two general statements:

1) God will judge those outside, that is, unbelievers. That is His responsibility.

2) The church's responsibility in any such situation is to put out the evil person from among its members. The verb

taken in the present indicative in the mode of an imperative implies immediacy. It is as if Paul were saying, "That's what you should do every time such a situation arises, and you should do it immediately."

The verb *exaírō* is derived from *ex*, "out of," and *aírō*, "to raise or lift up and away." The basic verb *aírō* implies the notion of violence and authority. It is spoken of cutting off or pruning branches as in John 15:2. It is also used in reference to removing out of the world by death as in John 17:15. Paul is instructing the Corinthian church and all churches in such instances to remove a wicked person out of the church. He tells them they have apostolic authority to do so and that they must do so no matter what the resistance. A wicked person who has fallen into the sin of fornication, and by extension all of the other sins enumerated in 1 Corinthians 5:10, 11; 6:9, 10, has no place in a Christian church since such sinners are strangers to God's kingdom.

Such a person whom the Corinthian church is asked to put away is called wicked. The Greek word is *ponērós*, "evil." The devil himself is called *ho ponērós* (see Matt. 13:19, 38; Eph. 6:16; 1 John 2:13, 14; 3:12; 5:18). The word stands in contrast to *kakós*, "bad in itself." *Ponērós* implies being not only bad, but also harmful. It is the opposite of *agathós*, "benevolent." In Matthew 5:45 the Lord said that "he makes his sun to rise on the evil [*ponēroús*] and on the good [*agathoús*], and sends rain on the just and on the unjust."

Why should the wicked or evil person immediately and resolutely be taken from among believers in the church? Because he can only bring harm. The discipline imposed, on the other hand, may have redemptive results in convicting him about his sin and convincing him that he cannot pretend to be a saint while living in sin.

Paul does not hesitate to call such a person by his proper descriptive name. This, however, should not cause us to conclude that Paul rejects this incestuous young man as an unbeliever. A believer who falls into sin does not become an unbeliever who needs to be saved all over again. He needs to be restored and he needs to realize the harmfulness of his actions.

Did not our Lord call Peter "Satan" when he tried to tell Him that He should allow His omnipotence to save Him from His necessary impending death on the cross (see Matt. 16:21–23)? This did not imply that Peter fell from being a disciple and became Satan.

Excommunication from the Church

What Paul was advising was excommunication which was used in the Old Testament. Ezra 10:8 tells us that the sentence against one who refused to part with his "strange wives" was that his substance should be confiscated and he himself separated from the congregation. Such a curse is mentioned as *anáthema*, "accursed," in 1 Corinthians 16:22 and Galatians 1:8 which probably involved a permanent exclusion from the church and possibly from heaven.

In the days of Jesus there were three forms of excommunication from the synagogue:

1) *Niddúi*, a short sentence of 30 days.

2) *Chērem*, which involved loss of all religious privileges for a considerable time.

3) *Shemmattā*, complete expulsion.

These Jewish forms of excommunication are referred to in the New Testament as follows:

John 9:22: "These words spoke his parents, because they feared the Jews: for the Jews had agreed already, that if any man did confess that he was Christ, he should be put out of the synagogue [*aposunágōgos*]," that is, he should be "excommunicated" from the synagogue.

John 12:42: "Nevertheless among the chief rulers also many believed on him; but because of the Pharisees they did not confess him, lest they should be put out of the synagogue" (see also John 16:2).

In Luke 6:22 another word is used. It is the verb *eaphorízō*, "to set off by boundary, to limit, exclude, excommunicate."

In Matthew 18:15–17 we may have a reference to some Jewish procedure that was taken over by the church. It involves first private admonition, then admonition in the presence of two or three witnesses, and finally in the presence of the whole church. The sentence "let him be to you as the heathen and the publican" involved loss of social and spiritual privileges (cf. Titus 3:10; 1 Cor. 5:4). The sentence in 1 Corinthians 5:5 was remedial and shows that it was not a life sentence as *anáthema*, "accursed," seems to be (cf. 1 Tim. 1:20). Interestingly, F. R. Montgomery Hitchcock in Hastings' *Dictionary of The Bible* points out that the word *exárate*, "remove," used in 1 Corinthians 5:13, suggests *ará* which means both imprecation or curse and prayer. In this case, he points out that the curse was intended to lead to penitence and prayer.

It is a certainty that the procedure adopted in the New Testament in the case of a believer in the church who has fallen into sin is that there should be separation, but such should be done in love and great sorrow. We must imitate Paul's example as he wrote, "Brethren be followers together of me, and mark them which walk so as you have us for an example. "For many walk, of whom I have told you often, and now tell you even weeping, that they are the enemies of the cross of Christ" (Phil. 3:17, 18). Let us never put out the erring brother by any other attitude but by weeping and prayer for his restoration.

Was the Incestuous Young Man Reclaimed?

From the indirect evidence we have in what Paul said in his later epistles, it seems most likely that this young man was reclaimed to the fellowship of the Corinthian church. From 2 Corinthians

2:1 it seems apparent that Paul wrote another strict letter to the Corinthian church which has been lost. It was alluded to in 1 Corinthians 5:9 and three times in the use of the verb "I wrote you" in 2 Corinthians 2:3, 4, 9. Paul wrote it with many tears (v. 4). He wrote it expressing great love for the Corinthians but great sorrow for the whole sordid affair. His criticism of them was not to condemn them, but to persuade them that he really loved them and wanted them to take appropriate action.

And then from verse five on he addresses another related problem, that of what to do with such a believer who had fallen morally and apparently repented. We are not definitively told he did repent, but we can conclude this by what Paul said in verses six and seven: "Sufficient to such a man is this punishment, which was inflicted of many." We have no information of any one individual who was censured by the majority of the believers of the church of Corinth. What is translated as "many" is *pleíones* which means the majority. This must refer to the majority of the believers who came at Paul's request to meet in the name of Christ to decide to deliver this incestuous young man to Satan so that his spirit would be saved (1 Cor. 5:4, 5). Apparently the decision was a majority decision but not unanimous.

What was the decision of the majority of the Corinthian church? The word is not *katadíkē* from *katadikázō*, "to condemn" as the UBS has it, or *díkē*, "sentence," implying punishment or punitive justice (see Acts 25:15). The word used in 2 Corinthians 2:6 is *epitimía* used only here in the entire New Testament. This noun derives from the verb *epitimáō*, "to admonish, reprove, rebuke." But none of these words truly conveys the exact meaning of the Greek words that are derived from the preposition *epí*, "upon," implying concentration, and *timḗ*, "honor," *or timáō*, "to honor." *Epitimía* is the concentration of the legal process to bring conviction to the accused or arouse in him a sense of honor leading to confession and repentance. It is to persuade him to consider how dishonorable his behavior has been to himself and his character so that he confesses and turns from it. In 2 Timothy 4:2 in the KJV, NASB, and the NIV the verb *epitímēson*, the aorist imperative of *epitimáō*, is translated "rebuke." However, more accurately periphrastically rendered it would be "arouse in them the sense of honor." When the Corinthian church met in Christ's name and with Paul's spirit being present, the purpose was to arouse in the incestuous young man a repentant sense of honor.

What Did the Minority Want?

There may have been some who did not want to appeal to this young man's honor that he was defaming himself and the whole church. This minority might have thought that such a man should irrevocably be thrown out forever and all redemptive counsel be cut off. They may have wanted complete disassociation. It may be that if and when the young man repented and wanted to be restored, this minority would object. Such a difference of opinion could bring division in the church. It is this situation that Paul addresses when in verse seven he writes, "So that contrariwise you ought rather to forgive him, and comfort him, lest perhaps such a one should be swallowed up with overmuch sorrow." Paul, in great wisdom, does not single out the minority dissenters, but the whole church. When there is division in the church of which there was plenty in Corinth (see 1 Cor. 1:12, 13; 3:5–9), one should not encourage it by pointing out the dissension, but should appeal for general unity.

It is interesting that the verb translated "forgive" is not the common *aphíēmi*, "to release from oneself, to send away from," but the verb *charízomai*, "to show grace, to bestow the undeserved status of grace." Although this man did not deserve to be restored to the favor of the church, can we say that any one of us deserves to be restored to fellowship with God after falling into sin? Only through the grace (*chắris*) of Christ can such restoration occur. This grace received by us must also be shared.

The absence of shared grace by believers in the church might have been disastrous to the individual who sinned, repented, and returned to the fellowship. To know that Jesus forgave him but that some of his fellow believers worshiping with him refused to do so could have caused overwhelming sorrow. Paul was pleading for sympathy toward this restored brother.

Thus in verse eight Paul writes, "Wherefore I beseech you that you would confirm your love toward him." That word translated "confirm" is *kurō̂sai* (aor. inf. of *kuróō*) meaning "to establish as valid, to give authority." It occurs only here and in Galatians 3:15. Paul wanted the dissenters to recognize that the love demonstrated, indeed worked. This ought to give them joy even if it proved them to be wrong in their possibly otherwise justified suspicion. One cannot argue with results. Now Paul pleads for the whole church to confirm their love to him. This is not easy to do for some self-righteous believers who think they are above others.

Martin Luther's Example

Martin Luther, being the great reformer that he was, could not help but also be a strict disciplinarian like the apostle Paul.

Before he nailed his ninety-five theses on the door of the church and while he was a professor at the University of Wittenberg, he learned that a monk studying at another university had gone morally astray. He wrote a letter to the prior of the monastery which epitomized his understanding of the pertinent teaching of the Paul in which he so lovingly expressed his concern:

> The sad news has reached me that one of my brothers from the monastery at Dresden has gone far astray and fled to you for refuge. I regret that the whole affair was so disgraceful. Nevertheless I am happy that

you were honorable and helpful in taking him in and have made it possible to end his shame.

He is a lost sheep and belongs in the fold. It is my duty to seek him out and turn him from the error of his ways, if the Lord Jesus be willing. I therefore beg you, most reverend Father and Prior, by our common faith in Christ and common oath to St. Augustine, if it is in any way possible for you to help, to send him back to Dresden or Wittenberg.

Persuade him to come yourself; treat him so kindly he will come of his own wish. I shall welcome him with open arms. He has nothing to fear. I am aware that great sins happen; it is nothing unusual when a man goes wrong. The miracle occurs when he comes to his senses again. An angel once sinned even in heaven. So did Adam in paradise. Peter fell. Every day a cedar of Lebanon topples to the ground. So there is nothing unusual if a reed is blown here and there by the wind.

The Temptation to Believe That We Cannot Be Forgiven

Verse eleven provides insight into Satan's devices. There is no doubt that it is he who tempted this young man to fall. Part of the blame may have been in the imprudent and indiscreet exposure of his stepmother, or even in her own sinful desires. We must be careful lest we help him along by causing others to be tempted to sin. But another victory for Satan is that often when we have repented and received forgiveness through the grace of the Lord, either Satan himself or even our fellow believers try to persuade us that our forgiveness is not real, that it is not enough. Having fallen into such hideous sin, Satan wants us to feel there is no way we can be fully cleansed and restored. In 2 Corinthians 2:11 Paul tells us, "Lest Satan should get an advantage of us: for we are not ignorant of his devices." The verb translated "should get an advantage of us" is the Greek *pleonektēthṓmen*, "to want more."[1] Satan gains a victory when he induces a believer to sin, but he is not satisfied with

1.The aorist passive of *pleonektéō* "to have more than one has had."

that. He is greedy. He wants more and that is to persuade us that when we receive Christ's grace it is not enough. He wants to convince us that our reputation is ruined and we might as well enjoy sin instead of seeking readmission into the community of saints. His ultimate victory is when he convinces other believers to doubt our salvation as being true and genuine. Satan can never have enough of us. He always wants more and more and he uses our fellow believers to exercise unforgiving pharisaism to discourage us.

Christ's grace is sufficient to turn fornicators, idolaters, adulterers, effeminates, homosexuals, greedy ones, thieves, drunkards, revilers, and extortioners into saints so that Paul in writing to the Corinthians could say, "Such were some of you" (1 Cor. 6:11). What could prevent the same grace from changing a believer who fell into fornication back to sanctity? Hebrews 8:13 states the unchanging character of Jesus by saying, "Jesus Christ the same yesterday, and today, and forever." Let us not allow Satan to take advantage of us by entertaining any hint that Jesus cannot restore the fallen saint who repents and turns from his sin.

> *A drop of water lay one day in a gutter, stained, soiled, polluted. Looking up into the blue of the sky it began to wish for purity, to long to be cleansed and made crystalline. Its sigh was heard, and it was quickly lifted up by the sun's gentle fingers—up out of the foul gutter, into the sweet air. Then higher and higher, until at length the gentle winds caught it and bore it away, away, and by and by it rested on a distant mountaintop, a flake of pure, white, beautiful snow! This is a little parable of what the grace of God does for every sinful life that longs and cries for purity.*
>
> —J. R. Miller

LESSONS:

1. Scripture forbids the total condemnation of a person regardless if the person concerned is a believer or an unbeliever.

2. A minister who preoccupies his time and energy with the sins of the word will not have the resources to watch over his flock. The apostles set the example ministers should follow by their preoccupation with discerning whether the behavior of those within the church was becoming to the teaching of Christ.
3. Paul's judgment of the incestuous man was not condemnatory of his character but rather an indepth evaluation and verification of his sin. Upon verification, every prayerful endeavor toward his repentance and reclamation to Christ and the fellowship of believers was to be made.
4. Those that are without are unbelievers, and those that are within are the church. God is the ultimate judge of all through Jesus Christ.
5. When there is division in the church, unity should be sought, and the gossip of any busybodies who point out the dissension should be stopped.
6. When believers try to persuade other believers that their forgiveness is not real, Satan has victory. Christians must remember that Jesus restores the fallen saint who repents and turns from his sin and that this alone is enough for the believer to receive the grace of the Lord.

Bibliography

Commentaries, Encyclopedias, Expository and Other Reference Works for English Readers

Alford, Henry. *The Greek Testament.* 4 vols. London: Rivingtons, 1880.

Chafer, Lewis Sperry. *Systematic Theology.* Vol. 7, *Pneumatology.* Dallas: Dallas Seminary Press, 1950.

Cremer, Hermann. *Biblico-Theological Lexicon of New Testament Greek.* Edinburgh: T. & T. Clark, 1954.

Grimm-Thayer. *Greek English Lexicon of the New Testament.* Edinburgh: T. & T. Clark, 1956.

Hastings, James. *A Dictionary of the Bible.* 5 vols. Edinburgh, Scotland: T & T Clark, 1901.

______. *A Dictionary of Christ and the Gospels.* 2 vols. Edinburgh, Scotland: T & T Clark, 1906.

______. *Dictionary of the Apostolic Church.* 2 vols. Edinburgh, Scotland: T & T Clark, 1951.

Hodge, Charles, *Systematic Theology.* Vol. 2. New York: Scribner, Armstrong, and Co., 1874.

Jelf, William Edward. *A Grammar of the Greek Language.* Vol. 2. London: John Henry and James Parker, 1861.

Kittel, Gerhard. *Theological Dictionary of the New Testament,* Vols. 1 and 2. Grand Rapids: Wm. B. Eerdmans Publishing Co., 1964.

Liddell, Henry George, and Robert Scott. *Greek-English Lexicon.* Oxford: Clarendon Press, 1958.

Perschbacher, Wesley J., ed. *The New Analytical Greek Lexicon.* Peabody, MA: Hendrickson Publishers, 1990.

Robertson, A. T. *A Grammar of the Greek New Testament in the Light of Historical Research*. New York: George H. Doran Co., 1923.

Trench, Richard C. *Synonyms of the New Testament*. Grand Rapids: Wm. B. Eerdmans Publishing Co., 1953.

Vine, W. E. *An Expository Dictionary of New Testament Words*. Old Tappan, NJ: Fleming H. Revell Co., 1966.

Lexicons, Encyclopedias, and References, for Greek Readers, from Classical and Koine Greek to Modern Greek

Byzantiou, S. D. *Lexikon tēs Hellēnikēs Glōssēs* (*Lexicon of the Hellenic Language*). Athens: Koromeela, A., 1852.

Demetrakou, D. *Lexikon tēs Hellēnikēs Glōssēs* (*Lexicon of the Greek Language*). Athens: Demetrakou, 1954.

Enkuklopaidikon Glōssologikon Lexikon (*Encyclopedic Glossological Lexicon*). Athens: Morfootikee Hetaireia.

Enkuklopaidikon Lexikon Eleutheroudaki (*Eleutheroudaki, Encyclopedic Lexicon*). Athens: Eleutheroudakis, 1927.

Kalaraki, Michael and Nikolas Galanos. *Iōannou tou Chrusostomou Ta Hapanta* (*Complete Works of John Chrysostom*), 1899.

Liddell, Henry George, and Robert Scott. *Greek-English Lexicon*, as Translated and Enriched by Xenophoon P. Moschos and Michael Konstan-tinides. Athens: John Sideris.

Megalē Helēnikē Enkuklopaideia (*Great Greek Encyclopedia*). Pursos (Pyrsos), Athens: Heelios.

Neōteron Enkuklopaidikon Lexikon Hēliou (*New Encyclopedic Lexicon "Heelios"*). Athens: Heelios.

Papaoikonomou, George L. *Lexikon Anomalōn Rhēmatōn* (*Lexicon of Irregular Verbs*). Athens: Kagiaphas.

Stamatakou, J. D., *Lexikon Archaias Hellēnikēs Glōssēs* (*Lexicon of the Ancient Hellenic Language*). Athens: Petrou Deemeetrakou, 1949.

Commentaries on First Corinthians Chapter Five

Aitken, W. Hay M. H. *The Highway of Holiness*. London: John F. Shaw and Co., n.d.

Alexander, Gross. *The Commentary and Homilies of St. John Chrysosotom on Galatians and Ephesians*. Grand Rapids: Wm. B. Eerdman's Publishing Company, 1956.

Allen, Clifton, J. *Points for Emphasis*. Nashville: Broadman Press, 1962.

Austin, William. *The Zondervan Pastor's Annual*. Grand Rapids: Zondervan Publishing House, 1965.

Aveling, F. W. "Discourses on Church History." In *The Christian World Pulpit* 14 (1878): 121-128.

Blair, J. Allen. *Living Wisely: A Devotional of the First Epistle to the Corinthians*. Neptune, NJ: Loizeaux Brothers, 1969.

Chalmers, Thomas. *Sabbath Scripture Readings*. Vol. 1. Edinburgh: Sutherland and Knox, 1848.

Cobb, W. F. *The Great Commentary of Cornelius 'A. Lapide*. Vol. 7. Edinburgh: John Grant, 1908.

Edwards, W. *Easter Meditations*. London: Arthur H. Stockwell, n.d.

Five Hundred Sketches and Skeletons of Sermons. New York: D. Appleton-Century Company, Inc., 1941.

Fleece, Allen G. "The Presence of Sin." *Seek*, 2, no. 3. Chicago: Good News Publishers, 1952: 7.

Forman, George. *Old Gems Reset*. London: Stanley Martin & Co., Ltd., 1930.

Frazier, Claude A. *What Did the Bible Mean?* Nashville: Broadman Press, 1971.

Golladay, R. E. *The Challenge of a New Day: The Epistles of the Ancient Church Outlines*. Columbus, OH: The Lutheran Book Concern, n.d.

Grubb, G. C., W. K. Campbell, and E. C. Millard. *Behold Your God*. Toronto: Bruce & Co., 1896.

Hallock, G. B. F., and M. K. W. Heicher. *The Ministers Manual*. New York: Harper & Brothers Publishers, 1951.

Hamilton, Mrs. Frank. *Bible Lessons in Bible Order*. Vol. 5. Chicago: Moody Press, 1934.

Hastings, James. *The Great Texts of the Bible*. London: T. & T. Clark, 1912.

______. *The Speaker's Bible*. Vol. 1. Grand Rapids: Baker Book House, 1962.

Hatton, Joseph. *Memoir & Sermons*. London: J. Gadsby, n.d.

Hawker, Robert. *Morning and Evening Portions*. London: Frederick Warne and Co., n.d.

Higley, L. H., Robert D. Higley, Arthur E. Bloomfield, John Paul, and J. A. Huffman. *Higley's Sunday School Lesson Commentary for 1941*. Butler, IN: The Higley Press, 1940.

Holden, J. Stuart. *Supposition and Certainty*. London: Thyne & Co. Ltd., 1930.

Horton, R. F. *The Apostles' Creed and Other Addresses*. London: James Clark & Co., 1895.

Jerdan, Charles. *For the Lord's Table*. London: Oliphant Anderson & Ferrier, 1899.

Keble, John. *Sermons for Easter to Ascension Day*. Oxford: The Society of the Holy Trinity, 1876.

Krutzky, Paul, and Carl Betz. *Themes for Vital Preaching*. New York: Doubleday, Doran & Co., 1929.

Landels, Dr. "Ritualism in the Services of the Church." In *The Christian World Pulpit* 4 (1873): 371-375.

Larson, Muriel. *Devotions for Women's Groups*. Grand Rapids: Baker Book House, 1967.

Lightfoot, John. *Hebrew and Talmudical Exercitations*. Vol. 4. Oxford: University Press, 1859.

Maclaren, Alexander. *St. Paul's Epistles to the Corinthians*. New York: A. C. Armstrong and Son, 1910.

Major, H. D. A. "Why Did Jesus Die?" In *The Christian World Pulpit* 117 (1930): 193-194.

McNeill, John. "The Pharaoh Bit in Men." In *The Christian World Pulpit* 116 (1929): 128-129.

McPheeters, Julian C. *The Epistles to the Corinthians*. Grand Rapids: Baker Book House, 1964.

Meyer, F. B. *Our Daily Homily*. London: Morgan and Scott, n.d.

Mitchell, Fred. *At Break of Day*. London: Marshall, Morgan & Scott, 1959.

Mitton, C. Leslie. *Your Kingdom Come*. Grand Rapids: William B. Eerdmans Publishing Co., 1978.

Morgan, G. Campbell. *The Westminster Pulpit*, Vol 5. Westwood, NJ: Fleming H. Revell Co., n.d.

Nicoll, W. Robertson. *300 Sermon Outlines on the New Testament*. Grand Rapids: Baker Book House, 1956.

______. *The Sermon Outline Bible: Acts 7—First Corinthians*. Grand Rapids: Baker Book House, 1958.

Perren, C. *Revival Sermons in Outline*. New York: Fleming H. Revell Co., 1894.

Plain Sermons. London: Gilbert and Rivington., 1845.

Raven, F. E. *Ministry*. Vol. 16. London: Stone & Cox Ltd., 1964.

Redpath, Alan. *The Royal Route to Heaven: Studies in First Corinthians*. Westwood, NJ: Fleming H. Revell Company, 1960.

Riggs, Elias. *Notes on Difficult Passages of the New Testament*. Boston: Congregational Sunday-School and Publishing Society, 1889.

Robertson, Frederick W. *Sermons Preached at Trinity Chapel, Brighton*. Vol. 2. Boston: Fields, Osgoods, & Co., 1869.

Roth, Samuel J. "Easter. 1 Cor. 5:6-8: Celebrate With Sincerity and Truth." *The Concordia Pulpit*. St. Louis: Concordia Publishing House, 1972: 133-137.

Schaff, Philip, and Henry Wace. *The Nicene and Post Nicene Fathers*. Vol. 12. Grand Rapids: William B. Eerdmans Publishing Co., 1956.

______. *A Select Library of Nicene and Post-Nicene Fathers of The Christian Church*, Second Series. Vol. 10. Grand Rapids: William B. Eerdmans Publishing Co., 1955.

Seiss, Joseph A. *Lectures on the Epistles*. Vol. 1. Philadelphia: General Council Publication House, 1915.

Simeon, Charles. *Expository Outlines on the Whole Bible*. Vol. 16. Grand Rapids: Zondervan Publishing House, 1955.

Smith, James. *Food for Hungry Souls*. London: Simpking, Marshall & Co., n.d.

______. *Handfuls on Purpose*. Grand Rapids: Wm. B. Eerdmans Publishing Co., 1955.

Spurgeon, C. H. *The Metropolitan Tabernacle Pulpit*. Vol. 16. Pasedena, TX: Pilgrim Publications, 1970.

______. *The Treasury of the New Testament*. Vol. 3. Grands Rapids: Zondervan Publishing House, 1950.

Stalker, J., and W. H. Hutchings. *The Sermon Bible: Acts 7—1 Corinthians 16*. London: Funk and Wagnalls Company, 1908.

Strang, M. W. "Christ Our Passover is Sacrificed for Us." *Words of Life*. Vol. 15. London: Elliot Stock, 1911.

Terry, Milton S. *Biblical Hermeneutics: A Treatise on the Interpretation of the Old and New Testaments*. New York: Phillips & Hunt, 1883.

Thomas, David Owen. *At the Lord's Table*. New York: George H. Doran Co., 1927.

Trueblood, Elton D. "The Christian and His Morals." *The Upper Room*, 1960. N.p.: 109-110.

Turnbull, Ralph G. *At the Lord's Table*. Grand Rapids: Baker Book House, 1967.

______. *This Business of Being Converted*. New York: Fleming H. Revell Co., 1942.

Vaughan, Charles John. *Sermons Preached in the Chapel of Harrow School*. London: John W. Parker and Son, 1853.

Wiersbe, Warren W. *Be Wise*. Wheaton: Victor Books, 1978.

Youngdahl, Reuben K. *Live Today*. Rock Island, IL: Augustana Press, 1959.

List of Abbreviations

acc. (accusative)
act. (active)
aor. (aorist [2 aor. for second aorist])
cf. (compare)
ch. (chapter)
comp. (composition)
dat. (dative)
etc. (and so forth)
ff. (following)
gen. (genitive)
i.e. (that is)
imperf. (imperfect)
indic. (indicative)
inf. (infinitive)
KJV (King James Version)
MT (Majority Text)
mid. (middle)
n. d. (no date available)
N. p. (no publisher available)
NASB (New American Standard Bible)
NIV (New International Version)
NKJV (New King James Version)
nom. (nominative)
p. (page), pp. (pages)
part. (participle, participial)
pass. (passive)
perf. (perfect)
pl. (plural)
pres. (present)
pron. (pronoun)
Sept. (Septuagint)
sing. (singular)
TR (Textus Receptus)
UBS (United Bible Society)
usu. (usually)
v. (verse), vv. (verses)
vol. (volume)

Guide to the Transliteration and Modern Pronunciation of the Greek Alphabet

Capital Letter	Small Letter	Greek Name	Transliteration	Phonetic Sound	Example
Α	α	alpha	*a*	a	as in father
Β	β	bēta	b	v	as in victory
Γ	γ	gamma	*g*	y	as in yell (soft gutteral)
Δ	δ	delta	*d*	th	as in there
Ε	ε	epsilon	*e*	e	as in met
Ζ	ζ	zēta	*z*	z	as in zebra
Η	η	ēta	*ē*	ee	as in see
Θ	θ	thēta	*th*	th	as in thin
Ι	ι	iōta	*i*	i	as in machine
Κ	κ	kappa	*k*	k	as in kill (soft accent)
Λ	λ	lambda	*l*	l	as in land
Μ	μ	mē	*m*	m	as in mother
Ν	ν	nē	*n*	n	as in now
Ξ	ξ	xi	*x*	x	as in wax
Ο	ο	omicron	*o*	o	as in obey
Π	π	pi	*p*	p	as in pet (soft accent)
Ρ	ϱ	ro	*r*	r	as in courage
Σ	σ,ς*	sigma	*s*	s	as in sit
Τ	τ	tau	*t*	t	as in tell (soft accent)
Υ	υ	ēpsilon	*u*	ee	as in see
Φ	φ	phi	*ph*	ph	as in graphic
Χ	χ	chi	*ch*	h	as in heel
Ψ	ψ	psi	*ps*	ps	as in ships
Ω	ω	omega	*ō*	o	as in obey

*At the end of words

SPECIAL RULES FOR THE TRANSLITERATION AND MODERN PRONUNCIATION OF THE GREEK LANGUAGE

COMBINATIONS OF CONSONANTS

Small Letter	Greek Names	Trans-literation	Phonetic Sound	Example
γγ	gamma + gamma	*gg*	g	as in go
γκ	gamma + kappa	*gk*	g	as in go
γχ	gamma + chi	*gch*	gh	as in ghost

DIPHTHONGS (DOUBLE VOWELS)

Small Letter	Greek Names	Trans-literation	Phonetic Sound	Example
αι	alpha + iōta	*ai*	ai	as in hair
αυ	alpha + ēpsilon	*au*	af, av	as in waft or lava
ει	epsilon + iōta	*ei*	ee	as in see
ευ	epsilon + ēpsilon	*eu*	ef, ev	as in effort or every
ηυ	ēta + ēpsilon	*ēu*	eef, eev	as in reef or sleeve
οι	omicron + iōta	*oi*	ee	as in see
ου	omicron + ēpsilon	*ou*	ou	as in group
υι	ēpsilon + iōta	*ui*	ee	as in see

BREATHINGS (Occur only with initial vowels)

(᾿) Smooth, not transliterated or pronounced.
When words begin with vowels, it may occur at the beginning of words with every vowel or double vowel (diphthong). ἔργον—*érgon*, work; εὐχή—*euchḗ*, vow.

(῾) Rough = h.
When words begin with vowels, it may occur at the beginning of words with every vowel or double vowel (diphthong). No distinction in pronunciation from the smooth breathing. To indicate the rough breathing we use "h" in the transliteration.

(ῥ) Rho = r.
(ὑ) Epsilon = u.
When these begin a word, they always have the rough breathing. There they are transliterated rh, hu, respectively. ῥέω—*rhéō*, flow; ὑπομονή—*hupomonḗ*, patience.

Scripture Index

Mark

Luke

John

Acts

Romans

1 Corinthians

Philippians

Colossians

1 Thessalonians

2 Thessalonians

1 Timothy

2 Timothy

Titus

Philemon

Hebrews